God of Deliverance and Transformation:

The Ten Commandments for the Twenty-First Century

Mark E. Diehl

$\mathcal{C}\kern-0.3em\raise0.2ex\hbox{$\curvearrowright$}$

Parson's Porch Books

www.parsonsporchbooks.com

God of Deliverance and Transformation: The Ten Commandments for the Twenty-First Century
ISBN: Softcover 978-1-949888-84-3
Copyright © 2019 by Mark E. Diehl

Dedication

This book is dedicated to Mary Brown Diehl, who has sojourned with me these past 40 years in unwavering grace, and, as my partner in ministry and best friend, is the source of my greatest joy.

Special thanks to the congregations who provided helpful response and critique to my initial offerings on the Ten Commandments: Pawleys Island Presbyterian Church in Pawleys Island, SC, and Unity Presbyterian Church in Fort Mill, SC. And thanks to my colleague Sara (Sally) J. Hughes for her interest and wisdom in putting into my hands *The Ten Commandments* by Patrick D. Miller: Miller's book provided the academic base to correct and verify assumptions I had made about the Decalogue and its meaning.

Contents

Preface

In a 1987 commencement address at Duke University, broadcast journalist and news anchor Ted Koppel entertained the audience with his observation about the Ten Commandments: "What Moses brought down from Mt. Sinai were not the Ten Suggestions. They are commandments." Unfortunately Mr. Koppel was wrong on both counts. In the Hebrew text, the translation is properly "words" or "sayings" rather than "laws" or "commandments." This part of the sacred text was initially referred to as the "Decalogue" or the "Ten Words" of God, and today some continue to choose the specific terminology of the "ten words" for its characterization.

Unlike most legal codes the "Ten Words" provide neither enforcement guidelines nor consequences for their violation. These "Ten Words" were the preamble to the Torah, the Jewish law, and became synonymous with legal requirements and codes of conduct among the Hebrews. In association with Jewish law, the Decalogue eventually was identified as the "Ten Commandments." Their character to guide behavior and to proscribe conduct was firmly established over the centuries and was wholly adopted by the Christian faith.

Unfortunately the Ten Commandments regressed, in the hands of some, into a coercive tool to establish and maintain control, and to enforce compliance. It is in this role that most contemporary audiences understand the commandments. That is why Ted Koppel and his listeners scoffed at the commandments being merely "suggestions." This is also the reason that many people today reject the relevance of the commandments in a multifaceted and diverse modern world.

The nature of the Commandments, however, need not reflect stringent codes of conduct or legal standards, much less abusive coercion. In fact, the Commandments provide a divine mandate to resist any authoritarian regime that enslaves people. In their original context the Commandments provide an alternative template to the coercion that previously served as the standard for the treatment of the enslaved. These "ten words" offer new possibilities and patterns for behavior, a vision to live into, with the goal of shalom, peace, wholeness, justice, and plenty for all. Instead of being requirements, these instructions serve more like the vows for marital relationships, taken on freely by couples, with the intent to guide and protect a growing and intimate bond.

Psalm 19 reflects the gracious understanding of Torah: "The law of the Lord is perfect, reviving the soul; the decrees of the Lord are sure, making wise the simple; the precepts of the Lord are right, rejoicing the heart; the commandment of the Lord is clear, enlightening the eyes; the fear of the Lord is pure, enduring forever; the ordinances of the Lord are true and righteous altogether. More to be desired are they than gold, even much fine gold; sweeter also than honey, and drippings of the honeycomb."

The purpose of this book is to restore an understanding of the Ten Commandments among contemporary audiences to this life-enhancing and gracious and revolutionary character. I also hope to encourage others to explore and discover and develop additional perspectives on the Ten Commandments for faith communities in the midst of the complex cultural realities in which we live.

Chapter One

The Ten Commandments for the Twenty-First Century

"I am the Lord your God, who brought you out of the land of Egypt, out of the house of slavery…." Exodus 20:2

"To be free is not merely to cast off one's chains, but to live in a way that respects and enhances the freedom of others." Nelson Mandela

With a good bit of trepidation, I offer this book on the Ten Commandments. How can a 3,000-year-old code of conduct written for people of the Iron Age be anything but unappealing for Twenty-first Century people in the Computer and Media Age? With this ancient scripture rehearsed and dissected and spoon-fed to generations before them, modern readers understandably resist new attempts to repeat this practice: "Oh, a preacher using the Ten Commandments to tell us what we should and shouldn't do! A root canal sounds more exciting. I definitely want sedation!" I don't blame you.

And should anything vital be found in the Ten Commandments, the voices of religious Zealots and secular critics alike will drown it out. Over the years the Decalogue has been used to impeach personal morality and, by guilt, coerce listeners into compliance with some version of religious rectitude. So the best possible outcome readers can anticipate for such a book is either to be bored to tears or to be assaulted by someone's aggressive religious agenda. It sounds fun either way, doesn't it?

Nevertheless Judaism and Christianity taught and preached and instructed the faithful productively, for centuries, using the Ten Commandments. Today, however, the Commandments have disappeared from many mainline Christian churches. Misuse by fundamentalists and secularists has led to reticence by many in the faith community to use them at all. I believe the Commandments are more robust than the shriveled moralistic crumb offered by some. Their relevance is more significant than the cultural battles about their display in, or removal from, civic and governmental locations in an attempt to shore up a nation's perceived religious decline.

So how do we find the value and vitality of the commandments in scripture? The first step is grasping the context in which the Ten Commandments were offered. The guidance found in the commandments was given to a previously oppressed and enslaved people, newly released and marching toward freedom. The Ten Commandments provided a transformative vision and path for life and wholeness, as well as divinely sanctioned resistance against any who would dominate and enslave humanity.

Today the idea of slavery is relegated to ancient history. Modern society and sensibilities are too sophisticated for such barbaric practices. However awareness is growing of contemporary manifestations of servitude and bondage: child labor, the sex trade, underpaid migrant workers intimidated by a fear of deportation, the young conscripted as soldiers. In addition, who of us cannot identify some form of subjugation in our own experience, be it institutionalized racism or sexism or addiction or mental illness that oppresses and confines?

Do people remain in need of deliverance today? And does the God who delivered the children of Israel from bondage intervene on behalf of the exploited now? Yes. The words of Exodus 20 are as relevant in the Twenty-first Century as when they were given: "I am the Lord your God, who brought you out of the land of Egypt, out of the house of slavery...."

If one were to read straight through Exodus 20, without any knowledge of the history of the Israelites before the commandments were given or how the commandments have been utilized in the centuries since, the Ten Commandments would appear relatively simple and straightforward. In reality they are vastly complex, and the truths they contain are nuanced and hidden from the casual observer.

Other moments of history uncover and disclose the nature of this complexity. One example is from a congregation I served in Fort Mill, SC. Unity Presbyterian Church was founded in 1788. Those settling in this part of the American frontier arrived from Great Britain, the land and country of their ancestors. They left a well-established pecking order, a caste system of hierarchy in which it was not only life-defining to know one's place but a matter of survival. Family alliances and rivalries circumscribed those to whom one could relate and how one was allowed to relate, be it as friend or foe.

They came to America to escape familial and societal and economic and religious restrictions that interfered with who they were and what they could become. And when they arrived in America, whom did they discover alongside them in this new world? Their neighbors from the old world, the ones with whom they had feuded in their ancient rivalries.

But now the old order with its dictates was gone. Other options existed that could be chosen to live differently. In a new world, a world of unknown promise and peril where their lives might depend on people down the road or in the nearby township, how would they negotiate relationships with their neighbors?

These immigrants chose for the congregation's name "Unity." According to the historical accounts, this name was selected because the settlers desired a different future without the divisions of the old world undermining their lives. So they bound themselves together in ways that established peace and promoted harmony and order.

Three thousand years ago, similar issues faced the Israelites as they made their way from slavery in Egypt to a new land and future. They had suffered under the whip of an oppressive regime that valued them for what they produced, not who or what they were. As a disorganized and diverse family of squabbling cousins, they were thrown together on a common journey. How would they choose to live? What would guide their life as a community to establish peace and harmony and the wellbeing of the community? The story of the Ten

Commandments is a tale of how the Israelites were guided to live into peace and justice.

In the present atmosphere of discord and division within and among nations in our world, I cannot think of a more apropos subject. However to delve into the Ten Commandments with the expectation of applying it to our culture today is fraught with difficulties. One cannot merely transfer 3,000-year-old rules and regulations for a fledgling theocratic nation-state of cousins into generalized principles for a democratic republic of diverse religions and nationalities and races and ethnicities today.

To make such an attempt is to invite disaster. For instance, the Israelites agreed to be governed by these commandments and renewed their commitment on a yearly basis. So today, do we merely impose these rules on all people in a specific geographic location regardless of their religious affiliation or preference in the matter?

And which version of the Ten Commandments would we use? More than one version exists. The Jews have one, the Roman Catholics and Orthodox have another, Protestants use a different one; Reformed and Presbyterian churches typically follow the Jewish version. Which is the "legitimate" one, or does it matter? And what about those people who do not follow the Abrahamic faith? Do they get a say? What about the founding principle in America of the separation of Church and State?

These conundrums only scratch the surface. Yet in spite of the challenges, I believe the Ten Commandments can speak to people of faith today, to inform and guide if we listen carefully and sensitively and faithfully. Our religious beliefs and practices need not be imposed on others in order for us to utilize the Commandments' insights and faithfully follow God.

The first words of this passage summarize the previous nineteen chapters of Exodus: "I am the Lord your God, who brought you out of the land of Egypt, out of the house of slavery...." Those chapters explain the predicament in which the children of Israel found themselves.

Jacob, his twelve sons, and their families settled in Egypt during the time of a devastating drought. They remained there, and through the generations, the families grew and became vast in number. Then a new king came to the throne in Egypt. Seeing the size and power of the Israelite community, he perceived these immigrants as a political threat. Their labor in the king's workforce was needed but he feared they might turn against him. This king, known as Pharaoh, shrewdly instituted a plan to gain greater control over them and enslave them. It worked. Ruthlessly the Egyptians imposed harsh physical labor as part of their effort to break the morale and collective power of the Israelites.

The Egyptians were winning this battle until a leader by the name of Moses intervened. Moses claimed to represent the Israelites and their God. In a series of confrontations with

Pharaoh, Moses created such disruption and chaos for Egypt that Pharaoh granted the Israelites' request to leave.

Upon their departure, Pharaoh changed his mind. His workforce and his economy were vanishing into the wilderness, so he pursued the Israelites with his armies. Pharaoh cornered them against the sea, but in a miracle of divine instigation, the children of Israel were delivered safely to the other side and the armies of Pharaoh were destroyed.

It is quite an epic tale, isn't it? I encourage you to read Exodus 1-19 to place the events in context and to understand the background.

The Decalogue begins: "I am the Lord your God, who brought you out of the land of Egypt, out of the house of slavery...." The God depicted here is not just any run-of-the-mill god that one uses like a good luck charm. This god is not the kind who might send rain when the front lawn needs watering or get you a parking spot near the front door of the market, or help your team win the Super Bowl. This god is not one who maintains the-way-things-are for the benefit of order and keeps everyone in his or her place insuring no one rocks the boat.

No, no, no. The God of the Israelites is a God who pulls parents and children and grandchildren out of an endless cycle of suffering and deprivation and hopelessness. The God of the Israelites dismantles institutionalized oppression and overbearing control intended to break the spirit of some and enrich the pockets of others. The God of the Israelites puts food in the mouths of the hungry and clothes on the back of the naked and sets them all on a path toward secure shelter in a land of peace and plenty. "I am the Lord your God, who brought you out of the land of Egypt, out of the house of slavery...."

The Ten Commandments provided guidance to people who had been slaves for 400 years. Treated as property, enduring centuries of oppression, generation upon generation living as though they were good-for-nothing ~ can you imagine how that affected their psyche? And now that they were free, how would they embrace the profound consequences of being human? How would they bear the responsibility for the success and failure of their family and community life, as well as the privilege of making voluntary and unforced choices?

The Ten Commandments are an adventure into how people of faith embrace God's deliverance and how that freedom requires transformation in their personal and social lives. It describes the moral and social structures necessary among those who respond to the remarkable grace of God. Those same issues impact the church and the world today.

As skeptical as you have the right to be, I hope you will travel with me this revolutionary journey through the Ten Commandments.

Chapter Two

First Commandment: Choose Carefully Your God: Your God Has Carefully Chosen You

"You shall have no other gods before me." Exodus 20:3

"God does not die on the day when we cease to believe in a personal deity, but we die on the day when our lives cease to be illumined by the steady radiance, renewed daily, of a wonder, the source of which is beyond all reason." Dag Hammarskjold

Do you know that everyone has a god? Even atheists do, although they wouldn't call it "god!" Everyone has a god. In every community and culture, some value or way of thinking or principle or power undergirds the choices made and the actions taken by people. The question is never "Do you have a god?" Rather the question for every person and community is "Who or what is your god?"

What determines good and right and truth and beauty for you? How do you tease out the ethical dilemmas of life and discern the most appropriate choices for resolving those quandaries?

You and I guide our lives and choices by a variety of authorities:

- Tradition, the way it has always been. At least until we find out it hasn't always been the way we thought.
- "Persistence and a good work ethic lead to success."
- "Today's science and technology open new vistas for humanity."
- "Go along to get along." "Don't rock the boat."
- "I believe in the Golden Rule. Whoever has the gold, makes the rules."
- "When you have your health, you have everything."
- "Marry rich."
- "When one door closes, another opens."
- "People are basically good."
- "Speak softly and carry a big stick."
- "Love conquers all."

Such perspectives reflect a loyalty to some belief system that guides us. And we learn our values and belief systems ~ what is authoritative, what works for us to keep us safe ~ we learn these from the people around us through our interactions with them.

Initially, this formative group is a small one consisting of our parents and siblings and extended family. As we get older that group broadens to include people from institutions of instruction such as church and school, and from social and cultural interactions.

Our experiences in these settings shape our expectations for life. They become norms that provide stability for us, that influence and impact our choices and responses.

The God of deliverance disrupted all the norms that had been learned by the Israelites during their 400 years of slavery. Generations of servitude to the Egyptian authorities ended and new possibilities began.

What god had they learned to serve in Egypt? "Go along to get along"? "Do only enough to get by"? "Suck up to your master"? "It's good enough for government work"? "Keep your head low and don't stick out"? How would those norms work in a new context in which they were free, where the value of their work accrued to the benefit of each person and their families and their community?

Centuries of oppression had taken its toll on their psyches, distorted what it meant to be human, and undermined the social structures that organized their community life. The children of Israel had to learn again what it meant to be human, how to make responsible choices for themselves, and how to live within a community as equal partners.

The Ten Commandments played an integral role in rebuilding the personal and social structures of a newly freed community of former slaves. The true value and worth of the Israelites as human beings were proclaimed and demonstrated in the words "I am the Lord your God, who brought you out of the house of slavery...." And having their humanity and worth affirmed, they then were prepared to hear the first words of instruction: "You shall have no other gods before me."

God's claim is an exclusive claim. No other force or power or influence or value will displace God. The exclusive claim is about who will be God, who in fact is God, who or what will act as an ultimate authority to those who are claimed by this God of deliverance.

The first word of direction to the Israelites from God is to trust this disruptive God of their deliverance. This disruptive God ended their slavery and provides freedom and promises an abundant future. Why would you trust some other god?

The reason why the Israelites would choose some other god is the same one we know all too well. We return to what is familiar, what has worked in the past, what is a habit. Have you ever tried to quit smoking, lose weight, or give up alcohol? Have you ever tried to forgive and forget? Have you ever tried to speak only positive things about other people? Our behavior is ingrained and reinforced, and difficult to modify, because at some point it helped us cope: to distract us, to mask the pain, to bring short-term pleasure. The god that delivered us in the past no longer works. And though this false god now has no power and effectiveness ~ it even may be counter-productive and destructive ~ yet we fall for its allure and false promises. Addiction works this way.

This intruding God of deliverance who now disrupts my oppression and sets me on a path toward freedom and wholeness and holiness ~ I don't know this God, I am not familiar with this God, I may not be able to control this God the way I want and expect.

I know what worked in the past; maybe it will work for me again. I return to habits of anger or drug use or dysfunctional responses to relationships. And so I fall into those patterns of behaving because I don't know any other way to be. I am comfortable with the familiar even if it fails me.

For some Christians, "what the Bible says" plays such a dysfunctional role. Even though they have never studied or perhaps even read the Bible, they claim the Bible as their authority. The Bible is not their authority at all. Instead their authority rests on what they "think" the Bible says, or what the loudest voice in the room insists that it says.

This first word of guidance from the Commandments is a word to be lived into: "You shall have no other gods before me." Other claims upon our lives must be abandoned. As the Old Testament scholar Patrick Miller suggests, the first commandment provides the basis for us to be truly human. We can only be truly human when we acknowledge our creator and accept the grace this creator gives us. We are called to say and believe, "God is our refuge and strength, a very present help in trouble. Therefore we will not fear." (from Miller, p. 29)

The characteristics of those who follow this commandment are twofold. One characteristic of the faithful is remembering God, recalling who is the source of all good and salvation and deliverance. By remembering, we combat the insidious tendency to forget God, to assume that any success we have is due to our own merit and is based on our own self-sufficiency, to believe that everything we have is because of our doing.

Another characteristic of the faithful is gratitude and thanksgiving, of celebrating our remembrance of God's goodness and grace through voiced expressions of appreciation and worship. Voiced remembrance helps us to properly attribute to God the benefits of our blessings.

"I am the Lord your God, who brought you out of the land of Egypt, out of the house of slavery. You shall have no other gods before me." Through the centuries, this disrupting, delivering God has chosen all who are beset by tyrants and tyranny, all who need rescue and deliverance. This disrupting, revolutionary God has chosen you and me. For those within the community of faith, the question is, "Will we choose the God of our deliverance?" Or will we choose other gods that lead down paths that may be comfortable or familiar or easy, even when those gods turn out to be the tyrants that terrorize us?

Chapter Three

The Second Commandment: No Substitutes Allowed

"You shall not make for yourself an idol, whether in the form of anything that is in heaven above, or that is on the earth beneath, or that is in the water under the earth. You shall not bow down to them or worship them; for I the Lord your God am a jealous God, punishing children for the iniquity of parents, to the third and the fourth generation of those who reject me, but showing steadfast love to the thousandth generation of those who love me and keep my commandments." Exodus 20:4-6

"A growing soul demands a growing thought of God; and mental images can be as stationary as marble or bronze. How perilous it is to carry in one's mind at twenty the same image of God that stood there at ten!" William Sloane Coffin, Sr.

When properly understood, the Decalogue directs God's people toward a quality of life that is full and fulfilling for individuals and for the community, and ultimately for the world. As mentioned before, the Ten Commandments have fallen out of favor. And often when the Ten Commandments are used today in the public sphere, it is at odds with the commandments themselves. Those who advocate the display of Ten Commandments throughout the land, perhaps depicted in stone or bronze in civic locations, are actually promoting a violation of the second commandment on which we now focus: "You shall not make for yourself an idol, whether in the form of anything in heaven above or that on the earth beneath or in the waters below; you shall not bow down to them or worship them."

The children of Israel took this prohibition seriously and continue to do so. Protestants in their earliest years likewise shunned the depiction of images of any kind, fearing that these images would become a focus of worship, potentially displacing God. Presbyterian houses of worship initially were simple structures devoid of ornamentation or decoration. Protestants have become less fastidious about such things in recent years, valuing artistic expression as a legitimate form of spirituality that can enhance worship and our understanding of God. Yet this commandment, which is the subject of our examination here, cautions us.

During my career I have encountered those who, self-identifying as people of faith, have allowed God to be displaced by other things. For one congregation, the predominating issue overshadowing all other concerns was the preservation and maintenance of the historic building. History and buildings and facilities are important! Yet this singular focus blinded them to other concerns properly part of their devotion to God: outreach to the hungry and homeless, developing programs of care for the hurting, utilizing facilities to teach adults and nurture children, worship.

Good things can deflect the faithful from the most important. The Bible, which contains the Hebrew and Christian scriptures, can become an idol. Devotion to flag or country can displace allegiance to God. In the Bible we see how religious people, good people, become distracted from the God whom they are to worship; they become preoccupied by the beautiful Temple, by their allegiance to the survival of their country, by riches and blessings. It becomes a tale of idolatry. Any "thing" or concept that displaces the God of deliverance and transformation by substituting something else in God's place is an idol.

Once upon a time, children in Sunday School were drawing pictures. One little boy had two figures in his picture. Even though his artistic skills weren't well developed, you could easily tell the two figures looked alike: same features, same color hair, same clothes. The only difference was that one figure was larger than the other. The teacher saw the picture and assumed it was of the boy and his father. But being a good teacher, she asked, "What are you drawing?" so that the child could explain the picture to her. Very proudly, the boy said, "It's a picture of God and me!" The teacher commented, "The two of you look very much alike." "Yes," the boy explained, "I made sure God looked good."

Whether it is the crude expression of a child with crayons or Michelangelo's in the Sistine Chapel, the outcome is always the same. We keep making God in our image, we make God look like us.

I remember my childhood days in church where the pictures of Jesus always had fair skin and blue eyes, just like all the children and parents in my community. Years later, I discovered that Christians from other cultures pictured Jesus looking like them: Africans had a dark-skinned Jesus, the Asian Jesus had features that looked like Asians. Humanity wants or needs or demands an affinity with a God, and the simplest way to establish that connection is through physical similarity. That is not necessarily a negative thing. The Christian tradition asserts this affinity in Hebrews 4: "For we do not have a high priest who is unable to sympathize with our weaknesses, but we have one who in every respect has been tested as we are, yet without sin. Therefore we can approach the throne of grace with boldness so we may receive mercy and find grace to help in time of need."

A cosmic force or power that transcends dimensional realities, that is not subject to time or the limits of space: to such a power humans struggle to relate. For the Christian faith, the incarnation of Jesus makes God accessible to humanity; Jesus becomes the embodied Word that can be heard and experienced and followed.

The problem is not that God makes accessible God's self to human beings. The problem is <u>when humans make God into what we think God should be</u>. In every case, such human endeavors reduce God, confining and constraining the Infinite. Ultimately such human attempts are ways to control and define and domesticate God, using God for our purposes rather than God using us for divine purposes.

As mentioned previously, a key to understanding the Ten Commandments is remembering the context in which they were given. These commandments are offered to freshly freed slaves who knew no other life than servitude and dehumanization. They had been subject to the whims of their masters and the all-powerful ruler of Egypt, Pharaoh, who acted as their god. As slaves in Egypt, their life and well-being depended on Pharaoh. But Pharaoh exhibited no care or love for the children of Israel.

Having escaped Egypt and tyranny, they now had nothing to guide them. Their masters and god (Pharaoh) were gone. Their slave labor that structured their day and directed their time no longer provided a pattern to organize their day or labor.

The commandments served to orient them, to remind them of a God who demonstrated concern for their welfare by their deliverance. The commandments provided a way to humanize each person and provide an ethic of care for all within the community.

This approach contrasted with the manner in which other gods were understood and utilized. Gods and idols of human making are for the purpose of human manipulation. Efforts directed to please these gods sought to win favor or gain blessing. Religious practice was to seize power or ascendency over others, whether it is our neighbor or coworker or the nation across the border. Gods made in our human image are assumed to operate on the same basis that we do: the same values, the same personality quirks, the same passions.

The God of Israel breaks these assumptions. Their God stood independent of human manipulation. This God is a just God, seeking the welfare of all, and in particular the oppressed. This God does not align with the powerful but with the powerless. The true and living God's intent is deliverance and transformation for the good of all.

So, what significance does this commandment have to people of faith, and how does it impact our lives today? What implications can we draw for its implementation in our present world?

First, this commandment alerts people of faith to examine critically and fully who or what has become our "God." Have we made God into our own image, and do we use our god for our own ends? Or are we reflecting the image that God has placed within us?

For the Christian community, the question is sharpened to this: Are we being conformed to the image of God in Christ? The best guides for discerning our "god" are to examine where our time and money and efforts are being directed; to see the fruits of the Spirit within our lives; to compare our focus in life with the focus of Jesus Christ in his ministry and teachings. Are we serving the living God who brings deliverance and transformation or are we serving the idols of this world? Is the love of Jesus Christ our focus by reaching out to heal and reconcile as he commanded, or are we withdrawing to protect ourselves and insulate our exposure to a needy world? Do we order people around or do we serve them?

Second, I believe this commandment has an impact on how we understand the diversity of humanity. When we make God into something that looks like us, we have placed boundaries on an infinite God who chooses to define and reveal God's self in whatever form God chooses. If God must look like us and like people from my culture or family, then those who look different from me are immediately suspect. I may perceive them to be threatening, maybe ungodly and evil. The threat and suspicion of the other, of the outsider, of the stranger comes precisely from making God in our own image.

To correct this problem, the Old Testament and Jesus provide many teachings about the obligation by people of faith to exercise special care for the stranger and outsider and alien. If all human beings are made in the image of God, rather than God being made in the image of me and people like me, then the diversity of the human family may serve as a corrective to our tendency to be tribal, excluding people of different races or ethnicity from our concern or care.

Third, this commandment suggests that God's image cannot be confined to some specific and never changing form. No matter how creative humans may be, no matter how gifted their talents, we cannot conceive or imagine God in God's totality. Therefore we must always be attentive to the fact that our understanding will be limited and faulty, and that God will exceed far beyond our expectations and limitations. Presbyterians express the reality of human inadequacy to fully comprehend an infinite God in the saying: "the church reformed, and always being reformed according to the Word of God." Our understanding should evolve as we mature and grow.

If your faith as a 35-year-old or 50-year-old or 70-year-old is the same as your faith when you were 10, something is wrong. Your faith has become rigid, fixed, inflexible. William Sloan Coffin, Sr. wrote many years ago, "The real difficulty of a graven image is its rigidity; it is fixed and therefore a limited and confining representation of God." (Coffin, p. 44) Anything that shares this rigidity in such a way that it will not allow itself to be reformed by God into a closer and truer representation of God's character and purpose, whether an object or our belief system, is an idol.

What are your idols that limit God's expressed image in every face that we meet in our world today? What idols are you keeping that limit the expansive and all-encompassing God of deliverance and transformation?

"You shall not make for yourself an idol, whether in the form of anything in heaven above or that on the earth beneath or in the waters below; you shall not bow down to them or worship them."

Chapter Four

The Third Commandment: God Isn't There for Your Advantage

"You shall not make wrongful use of the name of the Lord your God, for the Lord will not acquit anyone who misuses his name." Exodus 20:7

"Use what language you will, you can never say anything but what you are. What I am and what I think is conveyed to you, in spite of my efforts to hold it back." Ralph Waldo Emerson

The Ten Commandments serve as the bedrock of the Jewish and Christian faith, and when properly understood and used, they direct God's people toward that which preserves and enhances life. These benefits accrue not only to those who follow the Ten Commandments but also to any who engage with people of faith in commerce and society and civic interaction.

As we have seen, the Ten Commandments were given to a community of former slaves as they escape from bondage and progress to a promised land of self-determination. That journey of emancipation was not merely a geographical one; it was a moral and spiritual journey that encompassed the entire community: men, women, and children. To the extent that people of faith today want to traverse the journey from bondage to freedom, we must do so not only as individuals but also as a faith community committed to the God of our deliverance and transformation.

As the text from Exodus 20 demonstrates, God is the one who initiates the rescue of God's people. "I am the Lord your God, who brought you out of the land of Egypt, out of the house of slavery…" God makes a claim upon people, not only to deliver them, but also to transform them. And God transforms God's people by replacing the patterns of slavery, long etched in their souls and psyches, changing the habits of living as slaves in a system that cares nothing for their wellbeing. Transformative patterns of being are outlined in the Ten Commandments.

And so we have considered the first two commandments: "I am the Lord your God who delivered you: You shall have no other gods before me. You shall not make any image to represent me, to bow down and worship and serve an image that displaces me." Everyone serves some god or greater power, some principle or way of thinking. The God of Exodus requires those freed from slavery to continually choose the God of their deliverance who works for the well-being and common good of all. And secondly, they are not to make any image or representation of this God or any other god, for to do so is to limit and disguise and displace the God of their deliverance and transformation.

The third commandment follows closely in content to the first two as it continues its focus on the human obligation to God: "You shall not misuse the name of the Lord your God."

Another rendering of that commandment is "You shall not take the name of the Lord your God in vain."

A traditional interpretation and application of this commandment is the one found in polite society: "Don't cuss. And don't refer to God if you do cuss." And finally, "Whatever you do, don't cuss in the presence of a woman." In polite society, especially in the South, this is a most important commandment. It is what mamas attempt to instill in both their children and their husbands. In either case their efforts only meet with limited degrees of success. Despite this popular and common understanding, scripture's intent for the commandment has little to do with improving crass and unseemly conversation.

In the Old Testament, spoken oaths and solemn vows were used to secure commitments between people. In financial or property matters, collateral would be offered to guarantee that commitments were kept. If the vow was broken, the property could be confiscated to settle the dispute. But when the commitment involved a promised action or future consideration, there may be nothing of value useful in securing the promise. Examples of this include the sharing and division of inheritance property, treaties between countries, establishing business partnerships. In such situations, the integrity of the person making the pledge or vow, or commitment might be the only collateral available. Have you heard the expression, "A man or woman is only as good as his/her word"? A contemporary example of such a commitment is a marriage vow.

Unfortunately, humanity has a long history of piecrust promises as Mary Poppins would say, "promises that are easily made and easily broken." That was as true back in the ancient world of the Old Testament as it is today. In a world of lies and deceptions, how valuable is it to have some certainty that people are speaking the truth? That their promise is good and will be honored and fulfilled?

Years ago a village ironsmith had a reputation for being quite a religious man. A customer came in with a request for work. The ironsmith responded, "I will have it for you by Tuesday, God willing." The customer came in Tuesday, but the work was not complete. "I will have it for you by Thursday, God willing." The customer came in Thursday, but the work was not complete. The ironsmith promised, "I will have it for you by Monday, God willing." The frustrated customer responded, "If we keep God out of this, will you have it done for me by Monday?" God often gets the blame when we are the irresponsible ones.

Today we have contracts, either implied or written, codes of ethics, protocols that are followed: all guiding people to properly fulfill their obligations. Imagine how chaotic our world would be if testimony before a judicial hearing, or negotiated land boundaries, or the purchase and sale of property could never be reliably guaranteed, always subject to the risk of fraud.

In a community of ex-slaves where every single one of them had been extracted from bondage by the same redeeming God, the highest authority they could call upon to secure their commitments was to base oaths and vows in the name of the God of their deliverance. An oath made in the name of God placed on the line not only the reputation of the person making the vow, but also the reputation of God. Not to fulfill one's vows, not to speak truthfully in court, not to deal fairly with their neighbors and justly with business partners when their fidelity has been insured and collateralized by using the name of God: this was to take the Lord's name in vain; this was to misuse God's name.

To place God's name on something was to validate the veracity and truthfulness and value of that commitment or object.

To make vows invoking God's name was serious business for the Jews. God required that the Jews use only God's name to secure their vows, not the name of any other god or person. At the same time, the Jews were careful not to take the name of God upon their lips at all. To do so casually was to call upon God to validate their words as true when they might be speaking carelessly. The Jews considered that the truth of their speech might not live up to the same sterling character of association with God. So they cautiously avoided using God's name so as not to identify their thoughts and their words, which might be wrong, with God.

This reluctance to speak God's name is something that Christians could benefit from. Have you ever heard Christians claim that they know God's will? Something good happened, and so they assume it is God's blessing. Something bad happened, and we wonder what we did wrong.

There is a wonderful story from China that illustrates this challenge. Once upon a time there lived a man in a little home with his wife and son. Their only possession that amounted to anything was a beautiful horse, a mare in perfect condition. The neighbors always came by and said how blessed the man was to have this one beautiful mare.

One night the mare broke out of the corral; in the morning, the man discovered the mare gone. All the neighbors came by saying what a terrible thing it was to have lost the mare. About a week and a half later, the mare returned and with her she brought seven beautiful stallions. Following the mare, all the horses ran into the corral, and the man and his son closed the gate behind them.

Now they now had eight horses and all the neighbors came by and said what a blessing it was. The son decided to break the stallions in order to sell some of them. One of the stallions threw the boy and his leg was badly injured. The neighbors came by and said, "It is terrible that your son has hurt his leg." Not long after, the king of the country sent soldiers through the area to conscript all able-bodied young men for a war he was plotting. The son was rejected because of his injured leg.

All the neighbors' sons were taken away. The neighbors came over and said how lucky the man was that his son wasn't taken away to war because of his injured leg.

What is a blessing? To gain seven stallions? What is a curse? For a son to break his leg? How can we, not knowing God's grand design, claim to know God's intent and will in this immediate moment of time?

Over the years, I have heard many people claim they know God's will: Christians telling others what God's will is in very specific detail.

It might be the choice of a political candidate; it could be the intricacies of a particular policy. In every case, their declaration of God's will coincide with their own interests and perspectives. Have you noticed that?

In declaring what is God's will, they abandon caution by putting God's stamp of authorization on what they think is right. Such self-interested claims are taking the Lord's name in vain. Perhaps the most egregious use of God's name is to bless or curse a group of people, to elevate some for privilege and honor while denigrating others in order to devalue and dehumanize them. Any time people are devalued, God's image reflected in human beings is called into question.

This is a deep challenge for the church: speaking truth in love, confronting error with humility. We often get it wrong. One writer reflected on this challenge: "A Christian's entire life is named with the name of the Lord, the Lord of Truth: and a deceitful thought, the refusal to look at distasteful facts, the indulgence of what is recognized as prejudice, is to take the name of the Lord, our God, in vain." (Coffin, pp. 57-58)

In one church I served, we invited a Jewish Rabbi to speak about the Passover and its meaning for his community of faith. In telling the story and reciting the liturgy, the Rabbi included a prayer of mercy and forgiveness. It was immediately following the details about how the children of Israel crossed the sea on dry land and when the Egyptian soldiers followed, they were swallowed up by the waters of the closing sea and drowned. He offered a prayer of mercy for the Egyptian soldiers and commended their souls to God's tending. Instead of gloating, the Rabbi prayed for the enemies of his people. I was surprised and deeply touched.

The coarseness of our present public dialogue in demeaning opponents and demonizing their character in order to gain ascendency and win political battles is not new; but it has escalated to the point that the fabric of our common life as a nation is being torn apart by this toxic environment. To speak truthfully is to temper our words with humility before the God of our deliverance and transformation. We must not claim to know what God has kept hidden in mystery.

Abraham Lincoln struck this balance in the final words of his presidency. At the close of the Civil War in his second inaugural address, two weeks before his assassination, Lincoln attempted to draw together the shattered pieces of a war-torn nation.

He offered these humble words:

"With malice toward none; with charity for all; with firmness in the right, as God gives us to see the right, let us strive on to finish the work we are in; to bind up the nation's wounds; to care for him who shall have borne the battle, and for his widow, and his orphan--to do all which may achieve and cherish a just and lasting peace, among ourselves, and with all nations."

It is so easy to use God over against others for our advantage. We want to be right, and we want to get our way. Calling on God's name to achieve our own ends is to misuse God and God's name.

God's name is for the benefit and welfare of all people.

Chapter Five

The Fourth Commandment: Following God's Lead

"Remember the sabbath day and keep it holy. Six days you shall labor and do all your work. But the seventh day is a sabbath to the Lord your God; you shall not do any work – you, your son or your daughter, your male or female slave, your livestock, or the alien resident in your towns. For in six days the Lord made heaven and earth, the sea, and all that is in them, but rested the seventh day; therefore the Lord blessed the sabbath day and consecrated it." Exodus 20:8-11

"Judaism is a religion of time aimed at the sanctification of time. Unlike the space-blinded man to whom time is unvaried, iterative, homogeneous, to whom all hours are alike, qualitiless, empty shells, the Bible senses the diversified character of time. There are no two hours alike. Every hour is unique and only one given at the moment, exclusively and endlessly precious. Judaism teaches us to be attached to the holiness in time, to be attached to sacred events, to learn how to consecrate sanctuaries that emerge from the magnificent stream of a year. Sabbaths are our great cathedrals; and our holy of holies is a shrine that neither the Romans nor the Germans were able to burn…." Abraham Joshua Heschel

The fourth commandment completes and concludes the first section of Israel's obligation to the God of their deliverance and transformation. As we are continually reminded, it is imperative to remember that these commandments were offered to a community previously enslaved. The commandments' purpose was to transform the devastating effects of slavery etched into their souls and psyches for generations.

Many assume that the Israelites' escape from bondage meant they were free. Nothing could be further from the truth. The absence of the oppressor does not remove the internalized fear, the dehumanizing shame, or the pervasive sense of powerlessness. Flight from the whip of their masters does not remedy their anger at injustice, or the desire to strike out at those who perpetrated atrocities against their family. The psychic reverberations of slavery resound within every fiber of their being. Such debilitating reactions require transformation. To be truly free, former slaves not only must physically escape their captors; the internal emotional landscape must be transcended. Instead of reacting, they must choose to make responses to new circumstances that are life-giving and life-enhancing.

This is the paradox of faith: liberated from slavery, the children of Israel are now bound in covenant to their God. The Apostle Paul reflects this paradox in Romans 6:22: "You have been freed from sin and enslaved to God." Saint Augustine acknowledges the reality of this paradox in his prayer: "Help us to know you that we may truly love you, so to love you that we may fully serve You, whose service is perfect freedom." By following the Ten Commandments the children of Israel discover a path to transformation.

Before we proceed with this fourth commandment, I want us to take a little detour. It is related to the fourth commandment as the final one that completes the community's obligation to God before addressing their obligation to each other.

A detail provided in the story of God giving the Ten Commandment is that the commandments were inscribed on two tablets of stone. Scripture does not say which commandments were recorded on which of the stone tablets. Over the years scholars have debated a variety of opinions on the matter.

Some scholars conjecture that each stone tablet contains the entire set of commandments, resulting in 2 copies. This view is consistent with typical practice regarding agreements between two parties, with each party retaining a copy.

In a more traditional view, other scholars suggest that the first tablet contained commandments one through four which focused on humanity's obligations to God. You shall worship the Lord your God; you shall not make any idols or engraved images of God; you shall not misuse the name of God; and you shall observe the Sabbath set apart to God and cease all work in that day.

And according to these traditional scholars the second tablet held commandments five through ten, focused on humanity's obligations among themselves. Honor your parents; don't kill; don't misuse sexuality; do not steal; do not lie or speak that which injures your neighbor; and direct your desire for the good of your neighbor.

Whatever the arrangement on the tablets of stone, the commandments demonstrate the dual nature in a life of faith: our relationship with God and our relationship with neighbor. Both are required in a community formed by the God of deliverance and transformation.

The fact that the commandments focus first on the divine-human relationship might imply that those commandments are the most significant. Some people believe this to be true and spend a preponderance of their time cultivating an interior spirituality with God while neglecting human relationships.

Christian scripture instructs that how we treat others provides the true test validating or disqualifying our claim of relationship with God. I John 4:20 states: "Whoever claims to love God yet hates a brother or sister is a liar. For whoever does not love their brother and sister, whom they have seen, cannot love God, whom they have not seen." The way fellow human beings are treated is a demonstration of the quality of one's relationship with, and obedience to, God.

In situations where a conflict exists between fulfilling obligations to God and obligations to a fellow human being, Judaism provides specific guidance. The faithful are taught that "We must pursue our duties to the person, because the person needs our help, but God does not need our help." (Judaism 101: Aseret ha-Dibrot)

Jesus said this about the law: "You shall love the Lord your God with all your heart, and with all your soul, and with all your mind. This is the greatest and first commandment. And a second is like it: You shall love your neighbor as yourself." (Matthew 22:37-38) Jesus reflects the dual commitment of those who live a life of faith.

No separation of the first tablet of obligation to God from the second tablet of obligation to neighbor is legitimate. If by inattention or deliberate action, one of them is neglected, both have been destroyed.

So now we return to the fourth commandment: "Remember the sabbath day and keep it holy. Six days you shall labor and do all your work. But the seventh day is a sabbath to the Lord your God; you shall not do any work—you, your son or your daughter, your male or female slave, your livestock, or the alien resident in your towns. For in six days the Lord made heaven and earth, the sea, and all that is in them, but rested the seventh day; therefore the Lord blessed the sabbath day and consecrated it."

This commandment turns the eyes of the faith community back in time. Not back to their captivity in Egypt, not back to the days of their forefathers Abraham and Isaac and Jacob before entering Egypt, but all the way back to Creation. The fourth commandment returns us to the very purpose for which all humanity was created.

When Moses first confronted the tyrant Pharaoh, Moses asked that the children of Israel be allowed to step away from their burdens in Egypt in order to worship their God. Pharaoh rejected this request. Time is money: momentum would slow, progress would be delayed, and profits would be negatively impacted.

In a world where productivity and the bottom line are paramount, worship and rest and downtime are unaffordable luxuries. Pharaoh may get away to one of his many palaces, but a day of rest for common laborers is frivolous. So to put an end to such trivial requests in the future, Pharaoh doubled production quotas while increasing the required work. "If these Israelites have enough time to dream about being idle for a day, they have too much time on their hands!"

This is the tyranny of productivity, of business without ethical concern for workers, of devotion to getting ahead at all costs. To surrender one day for worship and renewal is radically countercultural in a world where our sense of worth and wellbeing are driven by what we produce and possess. The tyrant in whatever form he or she takes rises up and says, "NO! If you begin to believe that your worth and value are related to something other than the bottom line, the world as we know it will collapse." Worship is a royal waste of time to the gods that dominate this world.

People today have internalized this tyranny of productivity. When you slow down, do you get antsy? Are you deriving your sense of value from what you do? Is it challenging for you merely to be, to rest, to reflect, to assess, to gain perspective? Our internalized Pharaoh does not want us to relinquish productivity as the standard that determines our worth and value.

Sabbath intervenes in this depersonalization of human worth and cries "Halt!" The root meaning of the word sabbath is "stop!"

In all my years of ministry to folks who, in coming to the end of their life and reflecting on it all, not one has said, "I wish I had spent more time at the office." Not one. I have heard the words: "I wish I had spent more time with my family. I wish I had focused more on the kids. I wish I had taken more time for others. I wish I had participated in sharing the burdens of people in our community. I wish I had been more active in the ministry of the church."

Sabbath keeping in the Jewish tradition is one of their most prized practices, as well as one by which their faith is characterized and known. They have given the Sabbath such tender names as "Queen Sabbath" and "the holy, dear, beloved Sabbath." It reminds them and all who follow the observance of a Sabbath that God governs this world and grants meaning and worth; that the world is not completely dependent on humanity to make things come out right.

Do you believe the world rests on your shoulders? As difficult as it may be for us to comprehend, the world will not stop turning when you and I are gone. To practice Sabbath is to trust God. To observe the Sabbath is to put the world in its place. To honor the Sabbath is to return to the promise of creation, where even God upon whom all things depend, takes a day off.

Those reticent to surrender the preeminence of productivity to other values occasionally will make a concession to those insistent for a day of rest. Giving it a practical spin, they reason: "People will be more productive if they take time off to renew themselves." Abraham Joshua Heschel responds with a proper biblical and theological perspective: "Man is not a beast of burden, and the Sabbath is not for the purpose of enhancing the efficiency of his work" (*The Sabbath*). The purpose of Sabbath has nothing to do with productivity and everything to do with reorienting human life toward God. We are to remember <u>who</u> God is. We recall the words of creation, "In the beginning, God…" and in those words about creation, human beings are not mentioned until the very end. The Sabbath shifts the preoccupation and intoxication with human beings back toward God and our praise of God who is the source of all.

Marva Dawn is a contemporary Christian theologian who writes about worship. She embraces this perspective of the Sabbath centering our attention on God. After leading a service of worship, should someone comment to her, "I didn't much care for that second hymn we sang," she responds, "That's okay; we weren't singing it to you."

The fourth commandment also introduces a new element that becomes the focus of the remainder of the next six: our ethical obligation to others, to neighbors. The privilege of observing a day of rest belongs not merely to some: to one gender or to the wealthy or to the powerful. Sabbath does not belong to one race or nation. A day of rest belongs to all: children, workers, even aliens who sojourn among us. None are exempt.

By this broadly-based inclusion of all, an allusion back to creation is again made. Human beings are made in God's image, and that image is to be found in every person. Therefore, like God, all should rest. Precisely at this point, here in the Ten Commandments, the God of our deliverance and transformation provides the essential grounds for communities to embody tolerance and diversity and dignity for all.

The exploitation of slaves in Egypt has ended. No longer will such inhumanity be tolerated among God's people for the benefit of a few. The praise of God places all on equal footing.

"Remember the Sabbath day, to keep it holy. Six days you shall labor and do all your work. But the seventh day is a sabbath to the Lord your God; you shall not do any work—you, your son or your daughter, your male or female slave, your livestock, or the alien resident in your towns. For in six days the Lord made heaven and earth, the sea, and all that is in them, but rested the seventh day; therefore the Lord blessed the sabbath day and consecrated it."

Chapter Six

The Fifth Commandment: Assessing Our Blessing

"Honor your father and your mother, so that you may live long in the land the Lord your God is giving you." Exodus 20:12

"Our society must make it right and possible for old people not to fear the young or be deserted by them, for the test of a civilization is the way that it cares for its helpless members." Pearl S. Buck

The premise providing the foundation of the first four commandments is that human beings are dependent and interdependent creatures. Humans did not spring into existence as an act of their own will. The actions of others gave rise to our being. Our own initiative and exertion are only partially responsible for who we are and what we become. People of faith perceive God as the ultimate and originating source for the existence of humanity, and for what each person will mature into. Given this understanding, the obligation found in the first four commandments are not so much an "imposition" of obedience to the God of their creation as rather a reflection or expression of the reality in which people of faith live. Accepting these obligations is acknowledging with gratitude the source of our blessings.

The last six commandments are referred to as the second table of the Law. The last six focus on the horizontal dimension, the relationships among human beings. Like the first four, these commandments reflect our interdependent nature as social beings, products of families and cultures and societies that initiate our existence and influence what we become. As John Donne masterfully reminds us, "No man is an island."

Given the impossibility of bringing one's self into existence and living independently of others, the question then becomes "What will guide the nature and quality of those interdependent relationships?" The commandments thus reflect the dual nature in the life of faith: relationship with God and with neighbor. The commandments intertwine these realities and obligations of interdependence. People of faith cannot neglect or divorce one set of concerns from another.

Jesus insisted on preserving the dual nature of faith when he summarized the Ten Commandments. "You shall love the Lord your God with all your heart, and with all your soul, and with all your mind. This is the greatest and first commandment. And a second is like it: you shall love your neighbor as yourself."

And so we come to the commandment that introduces the second table of the Law, instructions which focus on human relationships. The fifth commandment centers attention on the most primal, fundamental and essential human relationship that exists in life: the relationship between a parent and child. It is a truism that the nature and quality of parent-child relationships will far outdistance the impact every other relationship a person will have during his or her lifetime.

The way that child values life, the way that child practices intimacy and fidelity with a spouse, the way that child cares for the possessions of others, the way that child speaks for the good or ill of others, the way that child masters the desires of his or her heart: the quality of response to these remaining commandments regarding interaction with neighbor is shaped by the nature and quality of the parent-child relationship.

Parenting responsibilities are overwhelming as it is. And the fifth commandment seems to enlarge them! Yet the impact of parenting carries societal consequences, which reverberate beyond the family and into the world. Faith communities play a crucial role in assisting families to shape the character and understanding of children.

About now, you might say, "I thought commandment five was about honoring father and mother, not about dumping responsibility on already over-burdened parents!" Fair enough! We must put it in perspective.

"Honoring" has to do with recognizing the benefits we receive from others. We honor God because God is creator and deliverer and sustainer, and our willingness to follow the Ten Commandments comes out of our response of honoring God for what God has done. Honoring parents parallels the honoring of God, as we acknowledge and enumerate the blessings that come from having parents in our lives, and as we strive to live up to their best ideals.

"Honoring parents" is more than mere acknowledgement of the biological reality that chromosomes have been contributed to a child, as important as that may be. "Honoring" does not require that one be a perfect parent, to be named "father or mother of the year." It has everything to do with the day-in, day-out struggle to love and discipline, to teach and maintain appropriate boundaries, to provide for bodily and emotional needs, to comfort and nurture. The most impactful actions by parents are to simply show up, be interested in and engage with their child. In spite of what some may claim, the highest "quality time" with children is inevitably "quantity time."

In Colossians 3:20-21, we hear the echo of children honoring parents and parents earning the respect of their children: "Children, obey your parents. Parents, do not provoke your children to anger so that they become discouraged." Usually we stop with the first phrase and direct it at our kids.

And when we hear the commandment "honor your father and mother," it is typically directed toward young children and youth to encourage their compliance. Occasionally it can be a lighthearted threat: "I brought you into this world, and I can take you out of this world!" Yet the reality of this commandment, as is true with all the commandments, is that its first audience is for adults. The force of this commandment, to honor father and mother, focuses on the honoring of older parents by their adult children.

The commandment does not mean to linger long into your adulthood with mom and dad by staying in their basement. It does not mean to return home if your first job doesn't work out. It does not mean to never disagree with your parents, or to assume all of their values, or to idealize them as though they were perfect. At the same time, neither should we become fixated on their failures. Parents are human. In regard to the imperfection of parents, one preacher insightfully pointed out, "For those of us who are still focused on the flaws of mother and father, it could be that those flaws are our best preparation for receiving the flawed relationships of the future." (Craig Barnes) If we have not worked through the often-tangled mess of parent-child relationships, it is likely that other relationships in our lives will be disordered.

The word "honor" means, "to make heavy." Another way of saying that is to give emphasis to or make significant, to focus on and take into account rather than to neglect. Honoring father and mother within Hebrew and Christian scriptures and traditions is not about offering words of praise. It has everything to do with demonstrating care and value and tenderness through specific actions. In the biblical context, it means the physical care of parents: their housing, their feeding, their health and well-being as they age. It has been observed: "the test of a civilization is the way that it cares for its helpless members." (Pearl S. Buck)

Jesus directed his criticism of the Pharisees in the seventh chapter of Mark on the basis of their refusal to obey the fifth commandment, to honor father and mother by caring for them. In biblical times when physical weakness and infirmity could leave persons vulnerable, the care of parents by the family took on great significance. It could be a matter of life and death. Society provided no safety nets: no Medicare or Medicaid, no nursing facilities existed in those days. In the cycle of life, the care of aging parents by their children was essential.

In addition, this model of honoring parents by caring for them provided a way of life to be emulated by the grandchildren and future generations. The adult children providing care to their parents will in time be the aging parents needing care from their children.

Joy Davidman writes about this dynamic in her book <u>Smoke on the Mountain</u>.

Once upon a time there was a little old man. His eyes blinked and his hands trembled; when he ate, he clattered the silverware distressingly, missed his mouth with the spoon as often as not, and dribbled a bit of his food on the tablecloth. Now he lived with his married son, having nowhere else to live, and his son's wife was a modern young woman who knew that in-laws should not be tolerated in a woman's home.

"I can't have this," she said. "It interferes with a woman's right to happiness." So she and her husband took the little old man gently but firmly by the arm and led him to the corner of the kitchen.

There they set him on a stool and gave him his food, what there was of it, in an earthenware bowl. From then on, he always ate in the corner, blinking at the table with wistful eyes. One day his hands trembled rather more than usual, and the earthenware bowl fell and broke.

"If you are a pig," said the daughter-in-law, "you must eat out of a trough." So they made him a little wooden trough, and he received his meals in that manner.

This couple had a four-year-old son. He was the light of their life! One suppertime the young father noticed his boy playing intently with some bits of wood and asked him what he was doing.

"I'm making a trough," he said, smiling up for approval, "to feed you and Mamma out of when I get big."

The man and his wife looked at each other for a while and didn't say anything. Then tears streamed down their faces. They went to the corner and took the little old man by the arm and led him back to the table. They sat him in a comfortable chair and gave him his food on a plate, and from then on nobody ever scolded when he clattered or spilled or broke things. (Smoke on the Mountain, pp. 60-61)

The community of faith knows they have been delivered in a multitude of ways in the weakest and most vulnerable moments of their lives. Through whom has that help come from our earliest and most tender moments? Parents are ideally the models for all caring and the ones God typically uses as instruments of grace within the lives of the young.

So our first ethical obligation is to those closest to us, who in our weakness gave us their strength, and now in their frailty relies on our strength. "Honor your father and your mother, so that you may live long in the land the Lord your God is giving you."

Chapter Seven

The Sixth Commandment: Protecting and Nurturing Life

"You shall not murder." Exodus 20:13

"Love looks beyond appearances.... Love has both the discernment and the imagination to see the whole person within the wounded person, the complex person lashing out behind the angry person, the gifted person living encased in the flawed person." William G. Enright

Under the thumb of Pharaoh in Egypt for hundreds of years, the Israelites were deprived of a basic sense of humanity, of proper dignity, of self-motivated responsibility. The only code of conduct that mattered for the enslaved children of Israel was that which Pharaoh offered, and its intent was to prosper the oppressor's projects and put profit into his coffers.

With deliverance led by Moses, the children of Israel were physically free from the oppression of slavery, yet its vestiges still clung to their psyche and behavior. The Ten Commandments initiated a process of transforming the children of Israel from the inside out. The first four commandments center on their obligations to the God of their deliverance; the last six focus on building a community of peace and justice and integrity.

It is important to consider the unique character of these biblical injunctions that pertain to the neighbor. As people in the 21st Century, we expect the commandments to instruct us to be responsible for ourselves. In that regard, the commandments disappoint us. Instead they clearly say, "You are responsible for the care of your neighbor." Honor father and mother. The life of your neighbor is in your hands. The marriage of your neighbor is your responsibility, to make it succeed. The possessions of your neighbor are your responsibility to safeguard, protecting them from loss. The good reputation of your neighbor is to be protected by the words you choose. The goodly gifts of life that belong to your neighbor you must not scheme to wrestle from them.

My neighbor's life, my neighbor's marriage, my neighbor's belongings, my neighbor's reputation: all of these are my responsibility, and your responsibility, according to the commandments.

The emphasis of this teaching is consistent with the earliest story found in scripture about Adam and Eve and their two sons Cain and Abel. Cain and Abel argue and Cain strikes Abel, killing him. Cain then encounters God who asks the whereabouts of his brother Abel.

Ashamed and defensive, Cain responds to God, "Why would I know where my brother is? Am I my brother's keeper?" In answer to every person throughout history who asks the question, "Am I my brother keeper, am I my sister's keeper?" the commandments affirm, "Yes. Yes, you are. You are responsible to protect them and, as much as it is within your power, to bring them good."

This is far more demanding than being told, "You must be responsible for yourself." It requires a significant commitment for us to be responsible for ourselves <u>and</u> for our neighbor. In such a community, it is not enough to assert one's own rights and defend against the abrogation of those rights, to demand equity, and to address one's own needs. In the community God is creating, antagonistic competition between one's self and one's neighbor cannot exist for long.

A man once asked God what the difference was between heaven and hell. God said, "Well, let me show you." God escorted the man down the hall and into a large room. In the center of the room was an enormous table set with plates stacked high with wonderful foods of every variety. Each person in the room had a fork; it was extra-long, so long in fact that it could reach any item on the well-stocked table, but it was too long to allow the person to eat the food off the fork. The room was chaotic and noisy as each person attempted to feed himself or herself, and all of them were failing. In the presence of all this table of plenty, the people in the room were malnourished and starving. God said, "This is hell."

God ushered the man out and then into the next room. Like the room they had just exited, an enormous table was set with all manner of foods. And also like the other room, each person had an extra-long fork that would not allow the food to reach one's mouth. The man turned to God: "This room is just like the other!" God smiled and said, "Look closer!" And when the man looked, he saw that each person with the long fork took food from the table; and though it would not reach his own mouth, the fork would reach the mouth of his neighbor. Every person shared with every neighbor what was wanted, and everyone had plenty, and no one was left out. The room was filled with laughter and conviviality, harmony and peace. No one went hungry.

The difference between every heaven and hell is always one of our making. The ethic presented by the commandments is that we proactively work for the good of our neighbor.

And when every person is working for the good of their neighbor, then all are cared for, all are cherished, all are protected, including ourselves. That is the intention and purpose of the commandments: to establish a community of shalom, of peace and justice. It is the very antithesis of every "me-first" society that in the end is merely another version of the land of slavery and oppression.

So now we come to the sixth commandment: "You shall not murder." Another translation says, "You shall not kill." Either statement seems straightforward and simple enough. Yet even in the choice of words for the translation from Hebrew to English, an interpretive decision has been made that nuances and impacts the meaning.

Murder is the unauthorized and premeditated death of one human being by the hand or action of another human being.

Killing likewise means to end the life of another, yet it is a broader term. Killing does not necessarily suggest premeditation or malice or an intention to harm in the way that the word murder does. The term "kill" allows for the possibility that the action may have been accidental or it was sanctioned by society or it was the expected course of events in nature. The difference between killing and murder is the difference between a lion who slays a wild hog for its dinner and a wife who extracts revenge on her husband because of his infidelities. Both could be called killing, but only one would be characterized as murder.

The Hebrew word translated in the sixth commandment can accurately be rendered as either "murder" or "kill." Communities of faith have understood this injunction as embracing the most basic reverence and protection for all human life. The first duty we have to our neighbor is to preserve and protect their life. Much like the Hippocratic oath of physicians, Jews and Christians in relation to all their neighbors are directed to do no harm.

The Jewish and Christian faiths reckon with the most brutal and barbaric of human acts, including murder. Our faith does not shy away from the condemnation of such destructive behavior. In later articulations of this commandment in the Torah, sanctions for killing are imposed based on extenuating circumstances. Like the legal system today, the Torah required testimony of witnesses, determination that the death was accidental or premeditated, and motive. The Torah also allowed the imposition of the death penalty for those convicted of capital offenses, as well as the authorization of killing in war.

Some claim a stricter meaning of this commandment in the rejection of the killing by anyone for any reason. Pacifism rejects an act of violence that might lead to death, including acts of war or state sponsored executions, and even self-defense. While this position is not strictly supported in the scriptural witness, it can certainly be argued on the basis of the life and teachings and model of Jesus.

Regarding this commandment, most of us can congratulate ourselves: "I haven't killed anyone today; not last week either; actually not ever. I'm doing pretty well with this Ten Commandment thing."

The challenge, as spiritual leaders and theologians through the centuries remind us, is not only about whether we have physically ended the life of another; it is about what we have done to promote and protect and make full the lives of others. The intent of the commandments is not to limit our liability but to embrace fully our responsibility.

For example, Judaism teaches that one cannot stand aside while another person's life is in danger. Some rabbis have gone so far as to suggest that one must avoid embarrassing others, because it makes the blood drain from their face, which is tantamount to shedding blood. That may seem far-fetched, yet Jesus confirmed it. Jesus said that abusive speech is like murder: "You have heard it said, 'You shall not murder.' But I say to you that if you are angry with a brother or sister, you will be liable to judgment; and if you insult a brother or sister, you will be liable to the council; and if you say, 'You fool,' you will be liable to the hell of fire." Jesus called this alternative approach "love."

Love transforms how we interact with others. As one writer says, "Love looks beyond appearances... Love has both the discernment and the imagination to see the whole person within the wounded person, the complex person lashing out behind the angry person, the gifted person encased in the flawed person." (Enright, p. 56)

C. S. Lewis speaks of the serious responsibility we have when we realize that in this world there are no ordinary people. It is "immortals with whom we joke, work, marry, snub and exploit." Every person has the potential to become "an immortal horror" or an "everlasting splendor" and how we treat them to some degree helps them reach one of those two destinations. (The Joyful Christian, p. 197)

Contemporary theologians observe that the great teachers of the church throughout the ages all agree that we are murderers when we fail to observe, "I was hungry, and you gave me no food or drink. I was a stranger and you did not welcome me; I was naked, and you did not clothe me." The Presbyterian Study Catechism (Presbyterian Church USA) frames the sixth commandment in this way: "we are to honor every human being." (Question 108) The valuing of human life as persons who reflect the image of God has encouraged communities of faith to embrace diversity within the human race as a divine gift, and to practice inclusion of those who are different from us. Violence is often the result of fear of the other, of those who are different.

In addition, the commandment "You shall not kill" leads the church to intervene in complex realities of contemporary society that kill people. Those realities include inadequate wages and unemployment, pension evaporation and skyrocketing medical costs, the lack of medical access for many, abortion, obsolete working skills and epidemic drug use.

If the church wants to become a peaceable community that takes to heart the commandment "You shall not kill," we must pursue the good of all people and learn how to make peace among ourselves and practice reconciliation. Achieving unity is not accomplished by silencing dissenting voices or pretending conflict does not exist. It is reached by weaving together a rich and multifaceted community through nonviolent resources such as confession, reconciliation, peaceful confrontation and forgiveness – resources that communities of faith have in their toolboxes of spiritual equipment.

Communities of faith are in the unique position to protect and nurture life, to advocate for the wellbeing of all, and to marshal the unique resources that are part of our traditions, in order to fulfill the intent of the commandment, "You shall not kill."

Chapter Eight

The Seventh Commandment: Protecting the Integrity of the Community

"You shall not commit adultery." Exodus 20:14

"Let us be honest with each other. The threat to marriage is not the gays. It is a lack of loving commitment —whether it is found in the form of neglect, indifference, cruelty or adultery, to name just a few manifestations of the loveless desert in which too many marriages come to grief." Malcolm Turnbull

The Ten Commandments are found in two different locations in the Old Testament and in two different settings. In Exodus 20, the commandments instruct the Israelites as they begin their long journey from Egypt through the wilderness to the Promised Land. In Deuteronomy 5, the commandments are rehearsed after the perilous journey as they stand on the doorstep of the Promised Land. While these two settings are substantially distinct and different ~ the prospect of an arduous road ahead versus the final crossing of home's threshold ~ the commandments remain essentially the same. The goal of the commandments remained the same: the creation of a community centered on the God of deliverance and transformation.

"The Promised Land" is what the children of Israel called the geographic destination of their journey from oppression in

Egypt. The spiritual and societal destination was called "Shalom" or "Peace." When one lives in tranquility with enough for all, in an atmosphere of justice and brotherhood, doesn't any place of residence become a land of promise? That reality is what countless communities of faith have found through the generations as they engage this story about a God who delivers the enslaved and transforms them into a peace-loving and goodness-seeking and just people.

Do ten commandments seem like too many? Most good speeches and sermons only have three points. God and Moses stretch the limits of good communication to the breaking point by making it ten. I remember a parent blurting out in frustration about the behavior of his son, "I can't think of all the things to tell him <u>NOT</u> to do!" Perhaps we should take comfort that there are <u>only</u> ten. In the legal instructions that follow the Decalogue, 613 additional laws are offered!

It was Martin Luther who said: "Anyone who knows the Ten Commandments perfectly knows the entire Scriptures." (from The Large Catechism) Jesus boiled the ten down to two: love God and love your neighbor. The Apostle Paul condensed it to only one. He said, "Love is the fulfillment of the Law." (Romans 13:10)

We now turn to the Seventh Commandment. "You shall not commit adultery." Like the sixth commandment, "You shall not murder," the seventh is straightforward and uncomplicated. However, unlike the sixth commandment where the meaning of the Hebrew word rendered "murder" can also be translated "kill" and therefore can be interpreted a variety of ways, there is no ambiguity about the term "adultery."

Adultery specifically refers to sexual activity that fractures commitments and vows made by those in a covenant relationship of marriage. Marriage provides an exclusive relationship with a mate. This covenant guards not only the marriage but the family of children produced by this union. The fifth commandment "honor your father and mother" protects the vulnerable aging members of the family. The seventh commandment protects vulnerable young members of the family as well as each partner.

Why might this commandment be needed? Think again about the situation from which the Israelites have just emerged: slavery. In any moment of history when the institution of slavery is practiced, the family structures of the enslaved are inconsequential. The relationship between husband and wife, the relationship between parent and child are irrelevant to economic and business interests. The bottom line is always more important than the welfare of slave families. As was practiced in the old South, so in Egypt with the Israelites: families would be separated on the basis of work and project demands and the need for laborers.

So, if the social structures of society do not reinforce marriages and families, how will they flourish? This commandment established the prominence of the family within the community and provided the grounds to advocate for those most vulnerable.

This commandment also played a moderating role within the patriarchal hierarchy that dominated that era. Men had the preeminent social position and a father's decision was considered law for all in the household. The wellbeing of women and children existed at the mercy and whim of men. As is true today, men in that culture generally had more mobility, resources, and privilege to go where they wanted and do what they wished. This reality made it simple for men to be promiscuous and engage in multiple sexual relationships.

In a social structure where men had the power and means to do almost anything, God speaks instruction that falls specifically to men to protect the most vulnerable among their kin. The commandment established grounds for challenging cavalier and irresponsible actions of the most powerful in society. The future of marriage and family life rested with men acting for the well-being of all.

This responsibility placed upon men did not work out so well. The story of King David is a case in point. You probably remember the story. While Bathsheba's husband was away at war, King David exercised his considerable power over the beautiful Bathsheba in a destructive act of adultery. David's lust exploited his neighbor for his own self-satisfying ends.

The incident escalated into the murder of Bathsheba's husband when David tried to hide his offense. David's deeds resulted in the destruction of his neighbors, not the care and wellbeing of his neighbors. When confronted by Nathan the prophet, David's abuse of power was what drew Nathan's condemnation: David took from the powerless and did not protect the vulnerable. (2 Samuel 12) Nathan's condemnation is the very rationale for the Seventh Commandment.

In the Twentieth and Twenty-first Centuries, women and children have made gains in legal rights and social protections; yet they remain the most vulnerable in modern society. The outcome of men's abandoning families is not so different today: the likelihood of family poverty, instability, and abuse remain. In every demographic, those at the lowest socioeconomic levels of our society are single mothers and their children.

The Seventh Commandment is often misunderstood today. People think, "I must not commit adultery in order to protect my own marriage and family." True enough: lack of fidelity in one's own marriage will inevitably destroy that most important of relationships.

However, the purpose of the commandments, as we have learned, is not to protect one's own interests. The intent is always first to care for our neighbor. "Do not commit adultery" is offered to protect the marriage and family of one's neighbor.

Did you know this was your responsibility? <u>Your neighbor's marriage and family life are given to you to preserve; you are</u>

to help it thrive. I cannot think of a more devastating and pernicious way to undermine a family's life than to disrupt the covenantal, exclusive sexual and emotional relationship granted and guarded in the commitment of marriage. So this commandment is not merely directed to married couples. It is to be attended by all within the community: never marrieds, young singles, widows and widowers, persons who are divorced.

The Seventh Commandment reaches far beyond what is narrowly cast as a private personal matter of fidelity between a husband and wife. We must ask ourselves as a community of faith as well as individuals, "What are we doing to help marriages and family life flourish?" We must take responsibility to uphold and encourage and undergird and build foundations for the long-term viability of marriage and family life.

A popular narrative today is to blame the decline of marriage and families on modern alternative lifestyles. However, I don't believe that narrative. The greatest threat is not a sinister agenda perpetrated by godless unseen forces. The greatest threat is not the legalization of same sex marriages or the independence of women and their rise in power. The greatest threat is the same one faced by Jewish society in King David's day when the most powerful took what he wanted without regard to the well-being of his neighbor.

Still today, we have King Davids who undermine the fabric of the family that lends strength to our society. The most powerful persons, even those in spiritual positions ~ people we admire and aspire to be like ~ are the ones who betray marriage. They say one thing in public but in private do something different. This threat to marriage comes from the arrogant and self-righteous and hypocritical: those who praise marriage to score political points but when their family life and relationships are examined, it is revealed to be a complete mess. The threat comes from those who defame and undermine the choices and practices of others while their own heterosexual dysfunctions and unbridled self-centered lust betrays the covenant of marriage as they move into marriage number three or four or five or six.

The most devastating powers that undermine marriage and family in any age are the unrelenting demands of Pharaoh, the powers that dominate our lives. The internalized "Pharaoh" who marshals our every whim demanding immediate satisfaction. Or the external "Pharaohs" whose abuse of power coerces compliance for whatever serves their own interests and gain. Throughout the millennia, internal and external Pharaohs have buffeted the human race. And the result is always the same: the basic structure that holds together our society, the family, is weakened.

Please note that this commandment provides no particular guidance or restrictions about human sexuality in any other setting than the covenant of marriage. Up to this point in the Biblical story, scripture portrays human sexuality in two ways. First, the Bible says that God made woman and man as they are, and God declared them "very good!" Human physicality and sexuality are positively affirmed. Second, the Bible indicates that sexuality is extraordinarily complicated and troublesome to mere mortals. That covers all of us. We must be careful to remain humble, to eschew arrogance, to be gracious, and to care for our neighbors.

Do you remember the story where a crowd of religious leaders, all men, brought to Jesus a woman accused of adultery? According to the Law, they insisted that she be stoned to death for her crime. However, there was a problem. The one person most culpable and capable of inciting adultery was the man, the male partner in this supposed crime. And he was nowhere to be found.

The Seventh Commandment, designed to protect the woman, was being perverted to destroy her. The religious people who were to care for and protect their vulnerable neighbor had become a mob seeking to kill her.

According to the story, Jesus bent down and wrote something in the dirt. No one knows what he wrote. Maybe Jesus penned a quote from Hosea: "I desire mercy and not sacrifice." Or maybe it was a word from Ezekiel: "A new heart I will give you, and a new spirit I will put within you... Then you shall remember your evil ways, and your dealings that were not good..." Perhaps Jesus merely wrote: "Where is the man?"

Whatever he wrote, Jesus then stood up and spoke, "Let the one who has no sin cast the first stone." And one by one, all the accusers left. Jesus remained. Jesus was the only one who cared for his at-risk neighbor.

"You shall not commit adultery." This commandment is not a call to safeguard our own marriages and families, and to stone those we perceive as threats. This commandment is a call to band together, to work for a community of love and peace and justice. This seventh commandment is a call to protect the most vulnerable of our neighbors ~ typically women and children ~ as well as any who are easily abandoned and abused by the powerful of this world.

Chapter Nine

The Eighth Commandment: Possessing and Providing

"You shall not steal." Exodus 20:15

"The bread of the needy is the life of the poor; he that defrauds them therefore is a man of blood, a murderer." Thomas Aquinas

L ike most of the commandments in the second Table of the Law, the Eighth Commandment is straightforward: "You shall not steal." To steal means to take for one's own use what properly belongs to another, and this taking is typically done by stealth or deceit. That is easy enough, isn't it? Such a moral standard would seem to be universally pertinent to all societies to maintain good order, and indeed such a standard exists everywhere.

As previously noted, the intent of the Commandments was to build a cohesive and peaceable community from the disparate and disorganized families that made up this fledgling nation. At this point in their sojourn, the children of Israel didn't even have land they could call their own. They were on their way to a land of Promise, but it would take them forty years to arrive and many more years to establish villages and communities and boundaries.

This commandment is a curious admonition directed to people who as recent slaves possessed little in terms of belongings. "You shall not steal." Do you notice in its brevity, that no object is mentioned? Later in the Torah, a variety of specific items would be named as examples of what should not be taken. Typically we would expect the list to be private possessions: in our day it would be cell phones or TVs or cars or jewelry; things like that. For the Hebrews, it was much more serious. It tied back to their history.

The children of Israel began their stay in Egypt when Joseph arrived there, hundreds of years before. It is in Genesis 40:15 that Joseph describes his arrival in Egypt: he explained that he was "stolen" out of the land of the Hebrews. His brothers kidnapped him and sold him to a band of nomadic traders out of spite and for spending money. Joseph's freedom was stolen from him for his brothers' profit. It ended well enough as all Joseph's family came to Egypt to escape a terrible famine. Over time however, a new regime ruled in Egypt, and they enslaved this growing population of immigrants that posed a threat to their power. Through devious means, again the children of Israel were stolen.

Look at all the things stolen from slaves: their labor, their wages, the use of their time, the capacity to worship, their choice of geographic location, their values, their families, their hopes. The greatest theft was their life and dignity and freedom. As one Biblical scholar has written, this commandment is "a specific and critical safeguard of human freedom." (Miller, p. 320)

We may find it surprising that the commandment, "You shall not steal," is a safeguard for human freedom. Many in America are unaware of the epidemic of human trafficking taking place in our own country and around the world. Recent news reveals incidents of foreigners lured to America with the promise of work and freedom only to be conscripted into the sex trade from which they cannot flee. The rich and powerful then take advantage of the plight of such immigrants in order to indulge their basest desires. "You shall not steal" is a safeguard for freedom and human dignity.

As the Hebrews developed their legal system after leaving Egypt, the most severely punished theft was the stealing of persons. Kidnapping and turning the victims into slaves was stealing life from another person for one's own profit. Other forms of theft required restitution from the thieves; the stealing of persons brought the death penalty.

Yet even commonplace stealing harmed and brought suffering to one's neighbor. In Jewish society, many people lived at a subsistence level, having just enough to get by. Laborers were paid at the end of each day so they could purchase food for their family. To withhold the laborer's wage was to steal from them and to place their family at risk. The legal codes protected the most vulnerable.

Through history, segments of society have lived on the edge, barely getting by. The theologian Thomas Aquinas in the 13th Century observed, "The bread of the needy is the life of the poor; he that defrauds them therefore is a man of blood, a murderer." It is still true today, from the working poor to middle class folks who live paycheck to paycheck. At the forefront of economic issues today are fair and living wages. Globalization, fair trade practices and protectionism, shifts in technology, movement away from manufacturing to a service economy, profit and productivity – all these impact the complex system that determine wages.

Ethical standards and business practices of major companies from pharmaceuticals to technology industries routinely surface as failing moral and legal requirements to protect workers, consumers, and investors. Such negligence always serves the purpose of lowering costs and increasing profits; and the perpetrators are rewarded handsomely. John Calvin, in the sixteenth century, observed that stealing "is made worse because often the thief is applauded. Indeed, he is not just applauded, but honored because he is such a big thief." (Stanley M. Hauerwas and William H. Willimon, *The Truth About God*, p. 107)

Perhaps you remember a company in the news in the early part of the Twenty-first Century. Enron was a huge energy and commodities company based in Texas, and everyone wanted in on the profits it was making, including financial institutions and investment funds. In 2001-2002, it was discovered that company officials had cooked the books. One of the big five accounting firms Arthur Anderson was implicated in the deception. $60 billion dollars was lost to investors, many of whom were retirees. The stock went from over $90/share to less than a dollar. 4,500 employees lost their jobs at Enron. The worldwide operation at Arthur Anderson went from 85,000 jobs to 2,000.

Immediately before Enron went bankrupt, 500 top managers collected sizeable bonus checks. When the CEO resigned, he collected $80 million in severance pay. Thousands of people around the world suffered because of this fraud, this theft. Many were left penniless in their retirement. Only 21 people were convicted or pleaded guilty to criminal charges. Concern for neighbor and the welfare of people around the world were ignored.

You and I lived through the great recession that is still dogging this nation and the global economy. It started with investors seeking profits off of bad mortgage loans; it ended with 8 million jobs lost in America, the stock market losing 50% of its value, and housing prices falling by at least 20%. Families were devastated financially as American households net worth declined 35%. The words "You shall not steal" are just as relevant a guide today as they ever were.

Petty theft on a smaller scale still does enormous damage to its victims, often the elderly and widow. In the Torah, the law protected such vulnerable people, requiring a cloak taken in pledge for a debt to be returned to a widow or orphan by the end of the day without regard to the repayment of the debt. In our world today, some might call keeping the cloak heartless but necessary. The Torah calls it stealing.

In the Hebrew scripture, the responsibility for the care of the poorest belonged to the community. Often the poor were the most likely to be targeted by thieves and other unscrupulous people. Contrast that to today when some within our society identify the needy as those who take advantage of, and take from, the rich.

Did you know that Nestle, a Swiss company, attempted to buy the rights to drinking water all around the world? It wanted the rights to water sources so it could profit from it. Ingenious, isn't it? Making water into a commodity so you can sell it to those who need it. And who doesn't need it? The CEO of Nestle claimed, "Access to water is not a public right." During a recent California water crisis, Nestle removed dwindling water supplies from the drought-stricken state to sell. Nestle claimed it was just good business. Five hundred years earlier, theologian John Calvin was prescient: if you are a big enough thief, people will admire your business acumen.

"You shall not steal" not only prohibits taking from your neighbor. It also carries with it a positive ethical requirement for doing good, taking care of your neighbor, and seeking their best interest. Jewish legal concerns over stealing even included this unusual situation. If you see your neighbor's animal has escaped its pen or is in distress, you are obligated to take action to help it and return it to your neighbor. The law is so specific that it says one must take these positive actions to care for your neighbor's animal even if you are at odds with the neighbor! (see Ex. 23:4-5, Deut. 22:1-4)

This foreshadows the words of Jesus: "You have heard that it was said, 'Love your neighbor and hate your enemy.' But I tell you, love your enemies and pray for those who persecute you, that you may be children of your Father in heaven."

The commandment not to steal carries with it an understanding of stewardship and the proper use of resources. How we manage and utilize natural resources impacts future generations. As it has been said, "We do not inherit the earth from our ancestors; we borrow it from our children." Ignoring the ecological implications of our actions today imperil generations to come. We hold all creation in trust for those to come lest we steal their future from them.

In the 1970s, environmental controls became necessary as the pollution of air and water and land reached toxic levels. The Environmental Protection Agency was a step to oversee the ecological and human impact of the unrestricted use of resources. Added to the business concern of profitability was the ecological concern for environmental damage and resource renewability and sustainability. Rolling back environmental protections solely to maximize profits for industry ultimately steals from the future of the human race.

The foundation of this commandment "You shall not steal" is built upon the First Commandment: God is the source of all, of creation, of our deliverance, of our life. We are called to be stewards of that life and use it for the benefit of all. According to this Biblical perspective, stealing from one's neighbor is not merely a violation of individual property rights; it is stealing from God.

Modern concepts of ownership and private property are at odds with Biblical understandings. One example is seen in the story of Jesus' triumphal entry into Jerusalem. Jesus instructed his disciples to find a colt in the village ahead and to bring it to him. If anyone questioned the taking of the animal, they were to say, "The Lord has need of it." In today's world, such a claim would be dismissed, and the person arrested for stealing. The Biblical understanding of ownership differs from modern concepts of private property and societal safeguards to protect individual ownership. For the Hebrews, the claim of God on possessions outranked the owner's claim because ultimately all belonged to God.

In the Christian community, the Apostle Paul reflects this biblical understanding in his instructions to the Ephesians. "Thieves must give up stealing; rather let them labor and work honestly with their own hands, so as to have something to share with the needy." The care of neighbor is the motivation: to contribute through honest labor to those in need. In a community that cares for one another and shares with those in need, the only motivation for stealing is to possess something exclusively for one's self. And in that grasping to possess, the thief exposes his god: the object of his theft, be it money or power or prestige or trinkets that glitter in the light.

"You shall not steal." To take this commandment seriously is to respond to the generosity of a gracious God, to address the pressing needs of those around us, and to tend the vast but fragile resources of creation for the benefit of generations to come.

Chapter Ten

The Ninth Commandment: Promoting Truth and Justice in Your Speaking

"You shall not bear false witness." Exodus 20:16

"Look at how a single candle can both defy and define the darkness."
Anne Frank

Up to this point in our examination of the Decalogue, we have found that the Commandments delineate specific actions and behaviors for the faith community to pursue or avoid. The purpose of these actions and behaviors is for God's people to live into, and nurture, a peaceful, harmonious, and just society. This society is in contrast to the one from which they were delivered in Egypt, an existence characterized by slavery, abuse, and humiliation. A purposeful existence and way of life was the goal for all people, not merely for a privileged few.

The previous eight Commandments detail actions that demonstrate the values of this God who has delivered them. These values include clarity of the source of authority that governs their new life, the preciousness of every person who is made in the image of the divine, the need of each person for rhythms of work and rest regardless of their social status, protection for the aged and the young and the vulnerable, and safeguards for the freedom and dignity of all persons.

So we come to the ninth commandment: "You shall not bear false witness against your neighbor." It is closely allied with the Third Commandment barring the wrongful use of God's name. The language here sounds borrowed from the legal profession and courtroom. Legal language was likely unfamiliar to former slaves who had little redress for injustices suffered and typically no standing in courts of Egypt. The fact that this commandment gives significance to their word and testimony and experience provided validation to their personhood and recently assumed position as equals within their newly freed community. Previously, justice for slaves was inconsequential, and it only occurred by accident if at all. So in building a new, free community, truth-telling and justice were critical components in forming social bonds that would maintain cohesion and promote peace and goodwill among the children of Israel.

Courts that hear disputes and attempt to make judgments on the basis of justice and fairness are dependent on truth-telling and are corrupted by lies. Inevitably a false witness undermines the character of another person by discrediting his or her statements. In many cases, perjury also leads to financial ruin, and in rare cases, the death penalty may be imposed on those targeted by lies. John Calvin made the broad and sweeping claim that "Whoever bears false witness against his neighbor kills him because he robs him and is guilty of whatever evil proceeds from his lie." (Sermons, p. 205)

Within its judicial setting, the Ninth Commandment reminds us of the power of our words. The reality is, however, that you and I frequently are uncertain that words have any impact on us.

Which is accurate:

- "Sticks and stones may break my bones, but words will never harm me"? Or "the pen is mightier than the sword"?
- Will "the truth will set you free," or is "talk cheap"?
- Is a person as good as her word, or is she a spin-doctor?

The Ninth Commandment confirms what is generally understood as a Hebrew concept, that words and actions belong together. Words and actions are distinguished from each other in modern societies that cherish the freedom of speech. Opinion may be protected speech, yet at the same time words can deceive or incite violence. Divorcing the power of words from the actions or reactions those words provoke is challenging. These distinctions are not merely academic in nature; they have life and death consequences.

Hate speech directed against specific targets often ends in violence against those people. If speech is the prelude to action, then hate speech demands immediate renunciation and response by society. The tragedies of the Christchurch New Zealand Mosques shooting, the Pittsburgh Tree of Life Synagogue shooting, and the Charleston Emanuel African Methodist Episcopal Church shooting are recent examples of this reality. Perpetrators of these rampages published hate-filled manifestos targeting Muslims and immigrants and Jews and Blacks prior to carrying out their atrocities.

It is easy to forget how powerful words can be, for good or ill. Words can reveal, and they can hide. Words can simplify, and they can confuse. Words can heal, and they can hurt. Words can create intimacy, and they can build walls of alienation. Words can stir the soul, and they can paralyze the body. If you have any doubt about the power of words, ask any parent who, waiting up for news from a child in the wee hours of the morning, picks up the phone and hears the words, "Momma, I'm okay."

The narratives of creation, which Jewish and Christian communities of faith utilize, reflect a God who speaks the universe into existence and by a word can make it flourish or wither away. God declared creation "good;" yet with demeaning words we tarnish God's image in our neighbor. For Christians, the Word is believed to have become incarnate in Jesus and is the source of all salvation. It is the witness of Christians, the words of testimony to our experience of life in Jesus, which the Holy Spirit uses to impact the lives of others. Am I a good witness or a false witness? Words matter to people of faith.

From this legal grounding of the Ninth Commandment to speak the truth, we also see the pernicious effects of lying as they snake their way into everyday life. Stretching the truth, offering half-truths, the lack of full disclosure, gossip, slander, flattery: all of these resonate with the commandment "You shall not bear false witness."

In our human experience, the breaking of the Ninth Commandment is typically committed in an effort to hide or deny responsibility for the contempt of such other commandments as stealing or killing or adultery. This constellation of disregard for the neighbor's welfare leads to the fracture of both our family relationships and those within the community among neighbors.

Within the Christian scripture, Ephesians says to "speak the truth in love." Could it be that if words harm our neighbor, then maybe they are not the truth? I know people, you know people, I have been that person and so have you: we handle truth like a weapon to wound our opponents in self-righteous love. One wise theologian has written, "We are bidden to speak the truth in love; and if we cannot speak it in love, we must keep silent." (William Sloan Coffin, Sr., p. 187)

Jesus cautioned his disciples: "Do not judge others so that you will not be judged." We never know what burdens others are carrying. We do not know their struggles, their disappointments, the challenges they face.

Unfortunately in the polarization of our society today, truth telling no longer is seen as a valued commodity. Many people demand agreement with their opinions or political positions. If you don't agree, you won't be allowed in their little circle, and your perspective will be dismissed.

Truth telling and integrity have become detached from each other. Uniformity of belief is more important than being allied with the truth. Real news is assailed by fake news and people can't tell the difference. Alternative facts are offered when real facts are embarrassing or inconvenient. An egregious lie carries more weight than an obvious truth depending on who says it.

Now, more than ever, we need to give heed to the words, "You shall not bear false witness." Truth cannot be determined by a majority vote. Speaking the truth in love occurs when reconciliation brings unity to all parties involved. The community must honor and work toward the wellbeing of all people.

The telling of lies is nothing new. These short-term fixes for difficult situations have been around for a long time. It was in Sunday School that a young boy gave his answer about the meaning of the Ninth Commandment. He stated clearly and formally, "A lie is an abomination to God, and a very present help in times of trouble."

Why do people lie?

- To hide wrongdoing and to escape punishment.
- To pervert justice in order to get a favorable outcome.
- To wound or hurt for revenge or retaliation.
- To gain advantage, and to curry favor.
- To avoid confrontation.
- To win friendship or influence with others.
- To protect others or ourselves from strong emotional

reactions. We seek that protection by deflecting the truth, either because we believe that someone else is not strong enough to handle the truth, or we are not strong enough to handle the other person's reaction.

The Ninth Commandment and the Hebrew and Christian scriptures offer another path and goal, speaking the truth for the benefit and wellbeing of our neighbor. Jesus said the truth will set you free, and for people traveling a path of deliverance and transformation, this is the course to which God directs us.

Yes, truth-tellers are not appreciated in a deceitful world. Many truth-tellers are ignored or belittled, some are silenced, a few are crucified. Tyrants have always been threatened by the truth; they take whatever steps are necessary to bend and control it or destroy it outright.

Yet even one life, as little as it may be, one life truthfully and lovingly lived can impact the world for good. That has been true all through history. It was Anne Frank who wrote, "Look at how a single candle can both defy and define the darkness." And the Gospel of John assures us "the light shines in darkness, and the darkness did not overcome it."

"You shall not bear false witness."

Chapter Eleven

The Tenth Commandment: Desire the Good for Your Neighbor

"You shall not covet your neighbor's house; you shall not covet your neighbor's wife, or male or female slave, or ox, or donkey or anything that belongs to your neighbor." Exodus 20:17

"You have made us for yourself, and our hearts are restless, until they can find rest in you." Augustine

The tenth commandment brings to completion instructions offered to the Israelites for building a community of trust and justice, peace and mercy. Freed from the depravations of slavery, they now were traveling to a land of promise and plenty.

Deliverance was the first step. This liberation came as a divinely orchestrated and miraculous gift. The next step was transformation: a continuous, ever-deepening and totally encompassing change within persons and communities, from the inside out. Transformation as a life-long challenge is a gift, too. The form of this gift came through instruction on how to proceed; it was found in words of guidance that illuminated the uncertain and shadowy paths ahead. The gift of transformation was the Ten Commandments.

The commandments provide a model to live into; they equip the community with wisdom and encouragement in the midst of the challenges and adversities of life. Transformation seeks to instill new patterns within individuals and in the community, offering templates that foster shalom and peace and prosperity for all.

These templates for living, articulated in the Ten Commandments, begin with a proper understanding of, and relationship to, the God who delivered them. "I am the Lord your God, who brought you out of the house of bondage; you shall have no other gods before me." These life paradigms conclude with words that require vigilance for protecting the neighbor's wellbeing. "You shall not covet your neighbor's house; you shall not covet your neighbor's wife, or male or female slave, or ox, or donkey or anything that belongs to your neighbor."

The first commandment encouraged proper desire, the desire for God. The final commandment cautioned against the desire for that which distracts and disappoints. In a way, the tenth commandment summarizes all the other commandments and moves the community's focus from outward actions and behaviors to the inner life, the life of one's heart and mind, one's desire and intent.

The word translated "covet" means "desire." Desire need not have a negative connotation. Consider these positive and life-enhancing desires: the desire to know and do God's will; the desire for greater knowledge and deeper understanding; the desire to develop talents of artistry and craftsmanship through practice; the desire to build positive relationships and work for peace; the desire to alleviate or prevent the suffering of illness. A thin line exists between desiring to make life better and grasping for that which does not belong to us.

When should we be content and satisfied? When should we strive for more? The temptation depicted in the Garden of Eden for Adam and Eve was the forbidden fruit. It was desirable in its appearance and its taste and its ability to make one wise. By eating it, one could become like God! In coveting, our intent shifts away from basic needs and the joy of living and giving; it shifts toward possessing and controlling in the belief it will make ourselves into something more: more significant, more important, more powerful.

As an antidote to the human tendency to covet, some philosophies and spiritual practices seek to extinguish desire. If we desire nothing, then we will not be charmed by our neighbor's possessions or prowess. This philosophy makes sense because conflicts with others are minimized if desires are eliminated.

Judaism and Christianity have never endorsed the attempt to banish desire. The dilemma of human life is the power of desire and its potential for both good and evil. That is the existential reality in which we live. As one theologian reflected, "Without desire we would cease to be human; without God as desire's ultimate end, we become inhumane." (Reinhold Hutter).

Desire may lead someone to find the next cure for cancer. Desire may also lead to the next terrorist insurgency.

St. Augustine reflected on his own misguided and restless search for God. The blind alleys of lust and hedonism brought him no ultimate joy or meaning or purpose. He reflected the reality of his search with these words: "You have made us for yourself, O Lord, and our heart is restless until it rests in you." Misdirected desire is a corruption of our desire for God. Its many false substitutes never satisfy our deepest desires.

So the last commandment brings us back to the first commandment: desire in its destructive form is really substituting another god for the God of our deliverance. To covet is to lift the gods of money or sex or power or possessions above God. To covet is to say, "I'm not sure God will take care of this for me. I'll handle this myself." To covet is to disregard appropriate boundaries for the wellbeing of our neighbor by scheming to take what properly belongs to my neighbor and use it for my own benefit.

To inwardly desire what belongs to the neighbor gives birth to intent. Intent germinates into a plan to seize, to possess, to claim and control. The commandment "You shall not covet" calls people of faith to observe and acknowledge, and ultimately discipline, not merely one's outward behavior, but the inward thoughts that lead to our actions.

Coveting is the internal process that inevitably leads to breaking other commandments that protect our neighbors:

you shall not kill, you shall not steal, you shall not defame and lie, you shall not commit adultery.

Jesus focused on this internal process rather than the external behavior when he taught, "You have heard that it was said, 'You shall not commit adultery.' But I tell you that anyone who looks at a woman lustfully has already committed adultery with her in his heart."

The center of the problem of coveting, of misdirected desire, is a trust issue. Will you take control and manipulate those things that are not properly yours to control? Have you substituted something less than God for God? Will you trust God to provide what you need?

Our interior life is the springboard of our actions. What preoccupies our minds dominates what we do. "As a person thinks in her heart, so she is." (Proverbs 23:7) "Where your treasure is, there you will find your heart." (Matt 6:21) The commandment about coveting is a heart and mind check for us.

A grandfather was talking with his grandson. "Two wolves are inside of us and they are always at war with each other. One of them is a good wolf. He represents things like kindness, bravery and love. The other is a bad wolf and he represents things like greed, hatred and fear."

The grandson thought about this for a bit and then asked his grandfather, "Which one wins?"

The grandfather quietly replied, "The one you feed."

The interior human struggle of coveting is an old one, as old as the faith narratives about the beginnings of time: Adam and Eve, Cain and Abel, Noah and the wickedness of humanity. Comparison is the thief of joy. Do the successes and attainments of our neighbors evoke celebration, or do they unsettle us? Which wolf are we feeding?

Coveting finds ever-new ways to disguise itself, whether it is investment portfolio performances or bitcoin bubbles or scams of the elderly. Clinging and grasping, possessing and controlling are not expressions of faith and trust. The desire for the good of all and the wellbeing of those around us is the hallmark for those who have been delivered from bondage and are being transformed. They are living with open hands rather than grasping hands. Keep your hands open to the God who has delivered you. Keep your hands open to the neighbor you are called to love.

A couple came to a minister for premarital counseling. Mike, the groom, was the first one to speak. "I am really, really nervous about this marriage."

Mike now has the bride's complete attention, as well as the minister. "No, no, you don't understand. It isn't that I don't want to marry you. It's that I'm terrified of losing you." Mike explained further: "I was a teenager when my mother died, and I barely survived the grief it was so great. And I love you even more. So I can't stand the thought that something might happen to you. I am terrified."

The minister was tempted to say, "Oh, you are young, and you'll be just fine, let's get on with planning the wedding." But the minister wouldn't promise something he couldn't deliver; he had officiated too many funerals for young brides.

The minister said, "You know, Mike, in my experience, 100% of all marriages come to an end. And you are not going to beat those odds. So let's get back to planning the wedding."

"Whoa, whoa, whoa. Wait just a minute! What do you mean?"

The minister continued: "100%, everyone of them, they all end. Some through divorce, some through tragic loss, but they all come to an end. Look, let's think about it this way. Here is the best scenario—the two of you get 60 years together, falling in love more deeply every day. Spectacular marriage, the greatest love story ever. At the end of these years, one of you is still going to end up placing the other into the arms of God in a funeral service, and that is going to tear your heart out. It's not just a matter of having 'a good run.' I've been at the graveside when they lay their loved ones in God's arms; they don't even know who they are anymore because half of them is gone. And that is the best scenario. It can't be better than that. Why do you want to go through all that?"

"So I say, give her up today. Let's get the loss over with on the front end. Do you want to spend every morning anxiously worrying about losing her? No, you don't want to do that. You want to give her back to her Creator today. Don't covet this woman. She was never yours; she never will be yours; she has always belonged to the God who made her. Place her back in the Creator's hands. Then when you wake up every morning and find her in bed next to you, you can say, 'Ha, ha, you're still here! This is great! We have another day! It wasn't promised but it is given! Let's be grateful for another day together!" (a story told by the Rev. Dr. Craig Barnes)

Living like that is living life, not with grasping fists, but with open hands: open hands to the God who delivered you and me; open hands to the neighbor we are called to love. Our restlessness must be quieted finally in the gracious and loving arms of God.

"You shall not covet."

Chapter Twelve

The Commandments and Love

"Hear, O Israel: The Lord is our God, the Lord alone. You shall love the Lord your God with all your heart, and with all your soul, and with all your might. Keep these words that I am commanding you today in your heart. Recite them to your children and talk about them when you are at home and when you are away, when you lie down and when you rise. Bind them as a sign on your hand, fix them as an emblem on your forehead, and write them on the doorposts of your house and on your gates. When the Lord your God has brought you into the land that he swore to your ancestors, to Abraham, to Isaac, and to Jacob, to give you—a land with fine, large cities that you did not build, houses filled with all sorts of goods that you did not fill, hewn cisterns that you did not hew, vineyards and olive groves that you did not plant—and when you have eaten your fill, take care that you do not forget the Lord, who brought you out of the land of Egypt, out of the house of slavery." Deuteronomy 6:4-12

"Nothing that is worth doing can be achieved in our lifetime; therefore we must be saved by hope. Nothing which is true or beautiful or good makes complete sense in any immediate context of history; therefore we must be saved by faith. Nothing we do, however virtuous, can be accomplished alone; therefore we must be saved by love. No virtuous act is quite as virtuous from the standpoint of our friend or foe as it is from our standpoint. Therefore we must be saved by the final form of love which is forgiveness." Reinhold Niebuhr

In the course of our examination of the Decalogue, we discovered a revolutionary vision and path offered for people moving out of oppression and into a new life of promise. The scars of bondage run deep in the psyches and souls of former slaves. The oppression need not be physical slavery: it could be psychological or economic; it might be an abusive relationship or drug dependence; perhaps it is self-destructive or anti-social in ways that compromise the wellbeing of one's self and others. Anything that interrupts wholeness and health and peace for anyone in the community impacts all and is a source of brokenness that needs mending. Theologically that brokenness is known as sin.

The stories of the Hebrew and Christian scriptures are about a God who delivers people from brokenness and oppression, and then guides and empowers them into a life transformed toward wholeness and holiness and peace. The narratives of people and communities, begun in slavery and sin, have a new ending. No longer victims, they now are survivors, thriving in fruitful ways that impact for good those around them.

The Ten Commandments begin the process of piecing together the various strands pulled apart by brokenness and sin as it affects a person's life or a community's identity. The two Tables of the Law pinpoint the focus of reconstruction: on relationship with God and on relationship with the neighbor.

The first four commandments direct people of faith to a coherent understanding and appropriate practice of having a vibrant relationship with God.

- Worship God alone who is the one bringing you deliverance and life.

- Don't displace God or substitute anything else for God, even if it may be good or powerful or effective.

- Don't use God or God's name or God's reputation to further your own ends.

- Follow the model that God demonstrated in creation, taking a Sabbath to rest and to remember and to give thanks. And everybody gets the day off, not merely a privileged few.

The last six commandments direct people of faith to proper understandings of what builds peace and wholeness within the community. These instructions target our neighbors' wellbeing, and therefore our own wellbeing. Cain asked the question that all humanity poses regarding the care of those closest to us: "Am I my brother's keeper? Am I my sister's keeper?" The commandments answer for all time: "Yes, indeed you are your brother and sister's keeper!"

The road to peace and justice, to a land of Promise and shalom, is a road not traveled in solitude but in community. And so these six commandments guide the people of faith in building community that is cohesive and resilient and fair:

- Acknowledge your debt and dependence on others, particularly your father and mother, honoring them with care and attention.

- Every life is precious and sacred: protect life.

- The most vulnerable in the family must be shielded from abuse and the family preserved.

- Do not jeopardize the lives others by stealing from them their liberty or their livelihood or their land.

- Do not rob your neighbor of their reputation by false speaking but pursue truth and justice in your words.

- Discipline the cravings of your heart and desire the best for your neighbor.

Christians apprehend in this God of the Decalogue the One revealed in Jesus Christ. References and allusions to the Commandments are scattered throughout the New Testament. Understanding the significance of Jesus' life and teaching is impossible without knowing the Decalogue. The most famous instruction of Jesus, the Sermon on the Mount, is patterned on Moses at Mount Sinai bringing the Law to the Jews. Conversations Jesus held with seekers and detractors frequently focused on the Law and its interpretation. To the extent that Jesus has any relevance to people of faith today, so also does the Ten Commandments.

Jesus simplified the Ten Commandments into two: love God and love your neighbor. Regarding the second Table of the Law, Jesus refined it to what is often called the Golden Rule: "So in everything, do to others what you would have them do to you, for this sums up the Law and the Prophets." (Matthew 7:12)

Taking his cues from Jesus, the Apostle Paul condensed the commandments governing our relationship with others to one command. "Let no debt remain outstanding, except the continuing debt to love one another, for whoever loves others has fulfilled the law. The commandments, 'You shall not commit adultery,' 'You shall not murder,' 'You shall not steal,' 'You shall not covet,' and whatever other command there may be, are summed up in this one command: 'Love your neighbor as yourself.' Love does no harm to a neighbor. Therefore love is the fulfillment of the law." (Romans 13:8-10)

Followers of Jesus Christ believe they are to love and embody love, consistent with the love demonstrated through the incarnation: "God so loved the world that he gave his son." One goal to which Christians aspire is to be conformed to the image and likeness of Jesus who gave himself, who served the needs of others, who sacrificed so all might have life. So at the very least, Christians are called to do no harm.

Yet today, in the name of God, some who identify themselves as people of faith harass and belittle their neighbor; some advocate legislating impediments to the full participation in society of those different from them; some obstruct the escape of families from desperate warfare and poverty and crime. Solutions to these challenging issues may be complex and controversial, but these issues cannot be ignored. One contemporary cultural critic (Cornell West) suggests, "Justice is what love looks like in public."

People of faith are called to do more than the minimum. While each commandment may prohibit a particular form of harm, these instructions also invite the faithful to positive and healing actions of support and nurture. When lives change for the better, new stories emerge that would never be imagined from their beginnings. Stories that begin in slavery become stories of hope and fulfillment and peace. Victimization no longer characterizes identity and predicts outcome. People become contributors to their families and communities, to the arts and to culture, to science and industry.

Informal organizations, nonprofits, and national agencies scattered throughout America in rural communities and urban centers make an impact one life at a time. The Children's Attention Home in Rock Hill, SC, provides a safe and nurturing environment for children who have been abused or neglected. Story after story can be told of children whose life experience began with heartbreaking and long-term victimization. Because of the loving and supportive presence and consistent guidance of people who care, a new future with productive and life-affirming possibilities is available to these children. It is a modern retelling of the Biblical story of deliverance and transformation. And this is not an isolated example; it is taking place all across America because people of faith know the power of love expressed in concrete deeds of intervention and help and healing.

Jesus suggested continuity between earthly acts of love and the heavenly kingdom. Painting a final judgment scene for his disciples, Jesus connected the dots between simple acts of care and help in the human sphere with the reality of God's Kingdom. "Then the righteous will respond to the King, 'Lord, when did we see you hungry and feed you, or thirsty and give you something to drink? When did we see you a stranger and invite you in, or needing clothes and clothe you? When did we see you sick or in prison and go to visit you?' The King will reply, 'Truly I tell you, whatever you did for one of the least of these brothers and sisters of mine, you did for me.'"

One purpose of the Ten Commandments suggested by Jewish and Christian theologians is its depiction of God's kingdom in the future, of the promise of heaven in paradise. If you want to know what the Kingdom of God looks like, study the Ten Commandments.

The Rabbis told in their stories that God's coming kingdom was disclosed in the Commandments. "At a time when God was giving the Torah to Israel, he said to them, 'My children, if you accept the Torah, and observe my commandments, I will give you for all eternity a thing most precious that I have in my possession.' 'And what,' asked Israel, 'is this precious thing which thou wilt give us if we obey the Torah?' 'The world to come – the world to come,' said the Lord. 'Show us in this world an example of the world to come,' says Israel. 'The Sabbath – the Sabbath is an example of the world to come.'" (Abraham Heschel, *The Sabbath*, p. 74)

A Christian theologian describes it this way: "We are led to the final function of God's commandments: they are descriptions of the life of the kingdom, which the church only anticipates. When we teach them to ourselves and to our children, this is the last and best thing we are to say: "God is making a world of love to God and to one another. See how fine that world will be. We will be faithful to God. We will be passionate for one another."""" (William P. Brown, *The Ten Commandments*, p. 18)

So the commandments guide the faithful into what ultimately, they will become in the presence of God, in the gracious and loving and peaceful kingdom of the One who delivers and transforms. More than legal requirements or a code of conduct, the commandments picture what God's people can be, and will be, together!

In a moving prayer, Christina Rossetti reflected this hope for the future delightfully confused with its present manifestation among God's people: "O God of patience and consolation: grant we ask you, that we may love and serve you and our brethren, and having thus the mind of Christ, may begin heaven on earth, until that day when heaven where love abides, shall no longer seem a strange and distant habitation to us."

Love begins in this life and continues on into the next. According to the Apostle Paul, "Love never ends." (I Corinthians 13:8) Yet love's presence and power continue to surprise us.

Within the African culture, a concept or worldview called Ubuntu is dominant in many of the tribes. This concept "embraces hospitality, caring about others, being willing to go the extra mile for the sake of another," according to Archbishop Desmond Tutu.

An anthropologist doing intensive study in African culture discovered for himself this concept. As he prepared to return to his homeland from Africa, he told the people with whom he was working, and who were now close friends, goodbye.

He was particularly fond of the children he had come to know. So the anthropologist brought a basket of fruit to share with them on his last day. On an impulse he decided to make a game of giving the basketful of fruit to them. He placed the basket near a tree, and then had the children stand a good distance away in a line. Teasing the children, he challenged them, "Whoever reaches the basket first gets all of the fruit!" The children lined up, and the man said, "Go!"

To his surprise, all the children joined hands and, together as a group, reached and claimed the basket of fruit. Sitting in a circle, they laughed and began to eat, sharing the fruit with everyone.

The anthropologist was shocked. He asked them why they ran together when the fastest could have claimed all the fruit for herself or himself. One child explained. "Ubuntu! How can one of us be happy if all the rest are sad!"

Leave it to the children to show us adults the way. (see Isaiah 11:6; Mark 10:13-16)

That is a picture of love and care and equity for all of us to live into. The Ten Commandments demonstrate the essence of love. Love embodies the God of deliverance and transformation, and love expresses what God's people are called to do and become.

A Note on Hermeneutical Decisions, Contemporary Scholarship and Bibliographical Resources

The interpretive approach employed in this study of the Decalogue embraces traditional exegetical and historical-critical methodologies, and contextual analysis. Present scholarship on the Pentateuch, and Exodus particularly, provides no definitive conclusions regarding authorship, dating of the text, audience to whom the text was directed, or the identity and specific intent of the redactors or editors in shaping the message or its placement in the narrative.

For instance, scholarly opinions regarding the major completion of the texts of Exodus range from the tribal period of the confederacy (1200 BCE) to the Persian period (550 BCE). An early dating places the narrative closer in proximity to the events of the Exodus and the founding of the confederacy, with the narrative thus providing insight into the theological themes undergirding the formation of the faith and the nation. A late dating provides interpretive possibilities for the narrative to be seen as theological reflection on the nature of exile and the hope of return to the Land of Promise. Themes of bondage, redemption, community building, and covenant with God (as portrayed in the Exodus narrative) are seminal reflections for the Jewish faith in both instances.

The lack of scholarly precision complicates the hermeneutical task, leaving the interpreter to say little for fear of getting it wrong, or to move forward with imaginative possibilities drawn from the text itself. Rather than saying little, I am choosing to use the received canonical text with its given (stated) context as found in the narrative. A redactor or editor was responsible for the narrative in its final (and present) form, providing a theological framework to be discerned and utilized by the community of faith. Contemporary situations of bondage, deliverance and redemption, personal transformation and community building, and covenant with God continue to resonate with this ancient story as faith communities reflect on such realities of life and what form faithful responses might take.

Scholarship that informs the content and assumptions of this study is drawn from the following resources:

The Decalogue and a Human Future: The Meaning of the Commandments for Making and Keeping Human Life Human, by Paul L. Lehmann, 1994

The Ten Commandments, by Patrick D. Miller, 2009

The Ten Commandments- The Reciprocity of Faithfulness, William P. Brown, 2004

Other consulted sources include:

Channel Markers, William G. Enright, 2001

Making Sense of the Commandments, Rupert E. Davies, Epworth Press (UK), 1990

The Sabbath: Its Meaning for Modern Man, Abraham Joshua Heschel, 1951

Theology of the Old Testament, Walter Brueggemann, 1997

The Ten Commandments, Henry Sloane Coffin, Harper & Brothers, New York, 1915

The Ten Commandments: A Study of Ethical Freedom, Ronald S. Wallace, 1965

The Truth About God: The Ten Commandments in Christian Life, Hauerwas & Willimon, 1999

Postscript

My hope for this book is to restore accurate understandings and appropriations of the Ten Commandments among contemporary audiences. The essence of the Ten Commandments is life enhancing, gracious and revolutionary rather than its modern depiction as being prescriptive or coercive. Paul L. Lehmann's book *The Decalogue and a Human Future: The Meaning of the Commandments for Making and Keeping Human Life Human* is an important guide and contribution to this discussion. It is equally my hope that others will be encouraged to explore deeper possibilities for non-coercive uses of the Commandments within faith communities and modern society.

Within Jewish and Christian liturgical observance, I believe rich and fruitful explorations are possible. The Jewish celebration of Pentecost (known as Shavu'ot) marks the giving of the Torah on Mt. Sinai. Deliverance from slavery in Egypt, combined with the ethical guidance of Torah, created opportunity for the family of Abraham, Isaac, and Jacob, now grown large, to find a common faith uniting them into a cohesive community. The Christian celebration of Pentecost appears unrelated to the Jewish celebration, merely a calendar coincidence. For Christians, Pentecost traditionally marks the giving of the Holy Spirit and the birth of the Christian church.

As distinct as are the celebrations of Pentecost among Jewish and Christian communities, explorations into their commonalities and themes should be pursued. The possibilities to examine include:

- the Biblical and theological connections between gifts of God in giving Torah and Holy Spirit, both which create/constitute a faith community;
- the nature of Torah and the Spirit in terms of their life giving and enriching characteristics as they illumine and guide the faithful;
- the deepening of social and ethical responsibilities in society for the people of God in receiving these gifts;
- the fantastical events associated with each event of "Pentecost" (as described in Exodus 19:16-19 and Acts 2:1-13);
- the expansive and inclusive role the gifts of Torah and Spirit have played to stifle exclusiveness and encourage openness in each faith community through time.

CPSIA information can be obtained
at www.ICGtesting.com
Printed in the USA
JSHW011404130322
23690JS00012B/150